City National Bank Cloquet & Carlton is pleased to make available this pictorial history of Carlton County. Our roots here are deep; our history enriched by the people we know and serve. It is our hope that this collection serves not only as a tribute to the history of Carlton County, but also as a symbol of expectation for an equally glorious future; a future marked by the continual pride we take in our families, schools, churches, and country.

❧ It is in this spirit we present to you this pictorial history. ❧

The Board of Directors, City National Bank
RODNEY P. THOMPSON, *President/Chairman of the Board*
DIANE HOFFMOCKEL, *Vice President/Director*
FLOYD RUDY, *Director*
TED MICKE, *Director*
DONALD SHEETZ, *Director*

City National Bank
Cloquet/Carlton

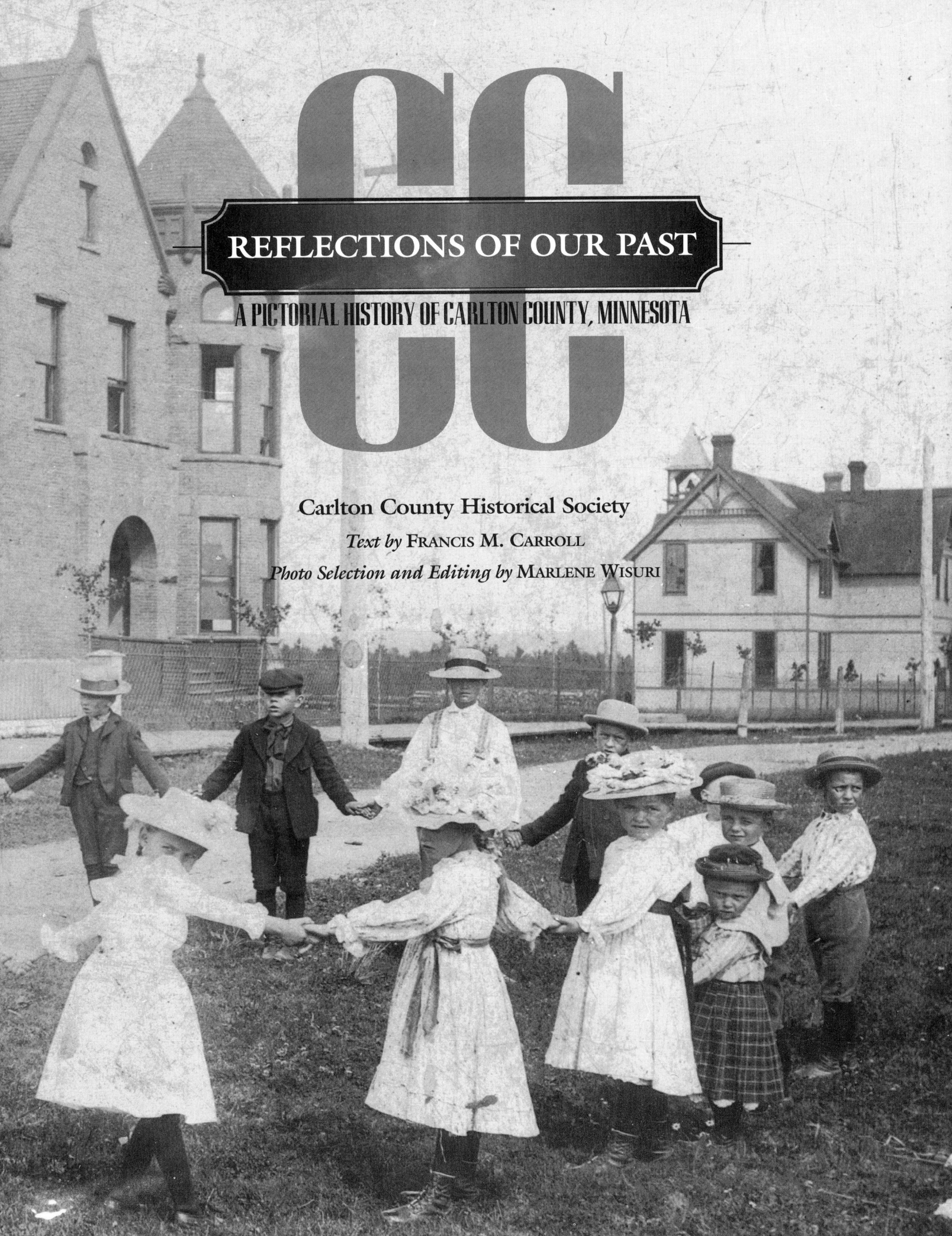

REFLECTIONS OF OUR PAST

A PICTORIAL HISTORY OF CARLTON COUNTY, MINNESOTA

Carlton County Historical Society

Text by FRANCIS M. CARROLL

Photo Selection and Editing by MARLENE WISURI

This book is printed on 80# Vintage Gloss text, made possible through a grant to the Carlton County Historical Society from Potlatch Corporation

ENDPAPER CUTLINE:

Map of Carlton County, M. J. Grindhem, McGill-Warner Co., St. Paul, 1944.

PREVIOUS SPREAD:

Children at play in late nineteenth-century Carlton County. A dance or a game or a fete? Beyond the picket fence is the new brick county courthouse, built in 1890 in the fashionable "Richardson Romanesque" style. The Carlton school is in the background. Boyer Brothers Studio photograph, from the collection of CCHS

Copyright © 1997 by Francis M. Carroll and Marlene Wisuri

All rights reserved, including the right to reproduce this work in any form whatsoever without permission in writing from the publisher, except for brief passages in connection with a review. For information, write:

THE DONNING COMPANY/PUBLISHERS
184 Business Park Drive, Suite 106
Virginia Beach, Virginia 23462

Steve Mull, *General Manager*
Nancy Schneiderheinze, *Project Director*
Paula J. Foster and Mary Downing, *Project Research Coordinators*
Dawn Kofroth, *Assistant General Manager*
Elizabeth B. Bobbitt, *Executive Editor*
Kevin M. Brown, *Graphic Designer*
Tony Lillis, *Director of Marketing*
Teri S. Arnold, *Marketing Coordinator*

Library of Congress Cataloging-in-Publication Data

Carroll, Francis M.
    Reflections of our past : a pictorial history of Carlton County, Minnesota / Carlton County Historical Society : text by Francis M. Carroll : photo selection and editing by Marlene Wisuri.
        p.   cm.
    Includes bibliographical references and index.
    ISBN 0-89865-991-4 (alk. paper)
    1. Carlton County (Minn.)—History—Pictorial works. 2. Carlton County (Minn.)—History. I. Wisuri, Marlene, 1940– . II. Carlton County Historical Society. III. Title.
F612.C15C38 1997
977.6'73—dc21   97-9724
                                                                                   CIP

Printed in the United States of America

CONTENTS

FOREWORD
by Hon. Lawrence R. Yetka 7

WORDS ABOUT THE PHOTOGRAPHS
by Marlene Wisuri 9

PREFACE
by Francis M. Carroll 11

ACKNOWLEDGMENTS AND ABBREVIATIONS 13

CHAPTER I
EARLY YEARS IN NORTHERN MINNESOTA 15

CHAPTER II
TRANSPORTATION AND THE
OPENING OF CARLTON COUNTY 27

CHAPTER III
THE WORLD OF FARMING 39

CHAPTER IV
WHEELS OF INDUSTRY 51

CHAPTER V
TOWNS AND SETTLEMENTS 65

CHAPTER VI
PEOPLE AND PLACES 79

CHAPTER VII
THE GREAT 1918 FIRES 93

CHAPTER VIII
RECREATION 105

CHAPTER IX
LIFE IN CARLTON COUNTY 119

FURTHER READING 139

INDEX 140

ABOUT THE AUTHORS 144

FOREWORD

Looking at a road map of Minnesota, or even driving through Carlton County, will not enlighten the visitor to the important role the County has played in the history of the Arrowhead region. This book will help tell the story. Carlton County was once one of the largest producers of lumber in the world and it is still a leader in the wood products industry. It is rich in Native American culture and leadership. Its white settlers came mostly from northern Europe. Finnish immigrants particularly likened the area to their native land and developed dairy farms, woodlots, and built their famous wooden barns and saunas.

Carlton County suffered severely in the Great Fire of 1918 which destroyed over 1500 square miles including the cities of Cloquet and Moose Lake. The fire was the greatest natural disaster in the history of the state. The courage and perseverance of the people who returned to rebuild the county inspired industry leaders of Cloquet to do likewise and to preserve the stable industrial base the city has always had.

The County's lakes, stream, and forests are hauntingly beautiful and although the climate admittedly is on the cool side, the residents have enjoyed fishing and watersports in the spring and summer, hunting in the fall, and winter sports in the heavy snow months of midwinter.

Many current residents of the County trace their heritage back to the last century. My own grandchildren are the fifth generation of my family to reside in Cloquet, and while my profession required me to live much of my life in the Twin Cities of Minneapolis and St. Paul, when I retired from the Supreme Court in 1993, I returned to my roots in Cloquet. I am convinced that it is a wonderful place to live and to raise a family. When you complete your study of this book, I am sure you will agree with me.

LAWRENCE R. YETKA
Retired Minnesota Supreme Court Justice

The offices of the BARNUM GAZETTE *and Post Office in 1904. The editor and staff stand by the door. Are the children "printer's devils" or the editor's children? From the collection of CCHS*

ABOUT THE PHOTOGRAPHS

This book is intended to complement the comprehensive history of Carlton County, CROSSROADS IN TIME: A HISTORY OF CARLTON COUNTY, that was published by the Carlton County Historical Society in 1987. It is a general overview of the county's history in photographs and graphics up to the time of World War II.

I have spent many hours pouring over the hundreds of photographs that are among the historic treasures of Carlton County. Many individuals shared their family collections for copying. These negatives have been added to the permanent collection of the Carlton County Historical Society and will be preserved for future use. The Esko Historical Society and the Moose Lake Area Historical Society have also contributed many photos from their collections. My biggest regret is that we couldn't use dozens more of these wonderful images. Wherever possible, I have tried to use photographs that were not previously published in CROSSROADS IN TIME or FIRES OF AUTUMN and that illustrate our history with the common activities of the people rather than formal "head shot" portraits or unpeopled buildings. In many cases I have had to use one or two images that are representative of activities that took place in all of the county's communities.

Because photographs can provide us with such precise detail from the preserved moment while still allowing us to bring our own memories and imagined stories into play, they are truly magical. I hope that you will enjoy this rich visual legacy that teaches us so much about our collective past.

MARLENE WISURI
Director, Carlton County Historical Society

PREFACE

Carlton County has a rich history. The stories of the Indian people in the region go back into the realms of myth and folklore. The written history of the region begins in the seventeenth century, the early years of French and English colonization in North America. In the late eighteenth and early nineteenth centuries, the county was centered in the midst of exploration, fur trade, diplomacy, and the assertion of American sovereignty over what is now called the upper mid-west. Although Carlton County took shape shortly after Minnesota itself was created, the county did not begin to grow with settlers and industry until after the building of the railroad in 1870. Rail connections with St. Paul to the south, Duluth to the east, and the building of the Northern Pacific straight west across the state opened up the county in the space of a generation. Indeed, within twenty years Carlton County was almost completely formed as it is today.

The year 1870, therefore, marks the beginning of a new era in the history of Carlton County and also coincides with the first photographs of life in the County. To be sure there were a few sketches and maps that have a more distant origin, but our visual impressions of life in Carlton County can almost be said to date from that moment in time when work began on the Northern Pacific Railroad on February 15, 1870. Looking at the photographs since that date one can almost see the county grow from a frontier settlement, clinging to the rivers and rail lines, to a mature society with a complex economy and a diverse population. This complexity and diversity gives the county much of its richness and interest. Add to that the beauty of the countryside and the closeness to nature that is still possible, and one has a promising subject.

This book is an introduction to the history of Carlton County, a visual introduction in fact. The photographs are just a few chosen out of the many considered. It is hoped that they will arouse your curiosity and make you want to see more. The text also is an introduction, which it is to be hoped will stimulate your interest, and here we can recommend CROSSROADS IN TIME and any of the very rewarding local histories that have been written about Carlton County.

FRANCIS M. CARROLL
Professor of History

Glasses of lemonade are enjoyed at the G.A.R. Headquarters after a warm march in the Fourth of July parade in Moose Lake in 1915. Fifty years after the Civil War, these Grand Army of the Republic veterans, Mr. Shaw and Mr. Webber, standing in uniform and with canes, would likely have been in their seventies. Girls in frocks and hats, boys in coats, ties, knee britches, and straw hats, are dressed to pay homage to the town celebrities at a patriotic occasion. From the collection of MLAHS

ACKNOWLEDGMENTS AND ABBREVIATIONS

We would like to thank Nancy Hanson and the Moose Lake Area Historical Society; Sylvia Siltanen and the Esko Historical Society; the research staff at the Minnesota Historical Society; Rodney Thompson and our sponsors at the City National Bank of Cloquet and Carlton; Potlatch Corporation, Northwest Paper Division; Judge Lawrence Yetka; Fern Olson, Archivist at CCHS; and the many people who so generously shared their family photo collections.

Abbreviations used in the Photo Captions:
CCHS - Carlton County Historical Society
MLAHS - Moose Lake Area Historical Society
EHS - Esko Historical Society
MHS - Minnesota Historical Society

Where the photographers are known, they have been listed first in the photo caption, followed by the collection or contributor.

CHAPTER I

EARLY YEARS IN NORTHERN MINNESOTA

LEFT PAGE:

Forest covered much of Carlton County in the 1870s. The spectacular white pines dominated, although other pines, spruce, cedar, and tamarack were found in abundance. Hardwoods, such as oak, maple, aspen, and birch grew throughout the county as well. From the collection of CCHS

In 1870 the Northern Pacific Railroad engineers called it Corona, the highest point along the tracks between Lake Superior and the Mississippi. Today Corona is only a sign along Highway 210 between the towns of Sawyer and Cromwell, but it has a place in the story of Carlton County. To the west and south rise a number of streams that flow south into the Kettle River and the St. Croix River and run to the Mississippi and the Gulf of Mexico. To the north and southeast are the beginnings of several brooks that flow into the St. Louis River and the Nemadji River that empty into Lake Superior and begin the journey through the Great Lakes to the St. Lawrence River and the Atlantic Ocean. Carlton County sits astride those two great waterways, south to the Mississippi and east to Lake Superior, and its history has been shaped by the opportunities that those two water systems provided. For Native people and then the fur traders, this watershed was of enormous importance, the route from Lake Superior to the interior of

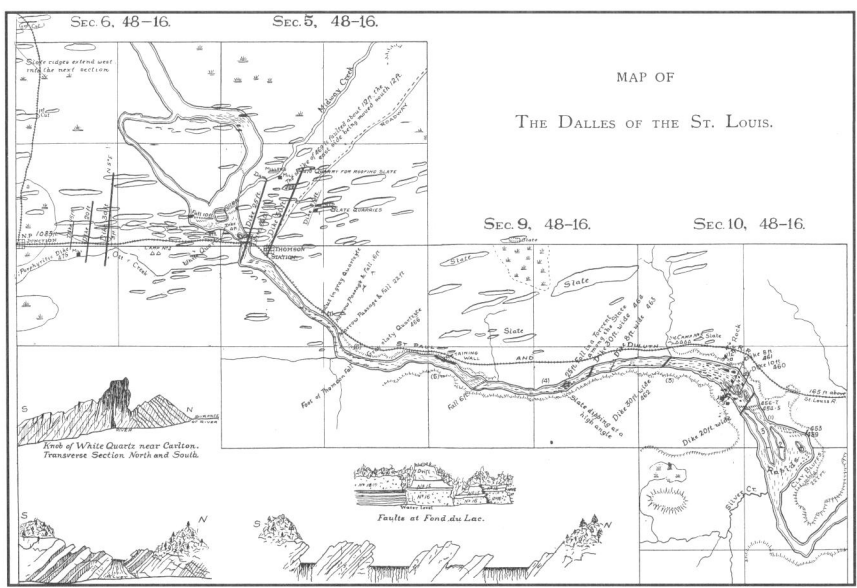

This 1890s geological map shows the lower St. Louis River from Thomson to Oldenburg Point. Of interest is the tracing of the St. Paul and Duluth Railroad, successor to the Lake Superior and Mississippi Railroad which was eventually merged with the Northern Pacific. The large island north of the falls is now submerged below Thomson Reservoir, as is the site of Andreas Miller's sawmill. From GEOLOGICAL AND NATURAL HISTORY SURVEY OF MINNESOTA, 1896–98

Shown here are the Fond du Lac signers of the Treaty of 1854 which created the Fond du Lac Reservation and ceded what is roughly Carlton County to the United States government. They are Frank Roy, Vincent Roy, E. Rousain, Frank Rousain, Peter Roy, Joseph Gourneau, and D. George Morrison, all names with long connections with the old fur trade companies. From the collection of the St. Louis County Historical Society

the continent. The St. Louis River was the gateway west and south to the Mississippi and north to the Rainy River and the Hudson's Bay.

By the early eighteenth century the Ojibway had replaced the Sioux in the western Lake Superior region. The Ojibway adapted well to the operations of the fur trade, and became themselves prosperous middlemen, trading first French and then English goods with other tribes to the west. The Ojibway of the St. Louis River had a life style apart from the fur trade, of course. Summer was usually spent at Fond du Lac, along the river, where corn could be planted and wild berries picked and preserved for winter. Fishing and hunting were easily accessible, and wild rice could be harvested. In autumn the Fond du Lac Ojibway moved up river to the site of the present Reservation for their winter encampment, and settled in smaller family units in bark wigwams in the woods. From these settlements the men hunted and trapped and the women made equipment and dressed furs. With spring, the families moved to the sugarbush to make maple sugar, after which they returned to the lower St. Louis River.

The Treaty of Fond du Lac in 1826 marked the beginning of negotiations between the Ojibway of northern Minnesota and the United States government. It was the policy of the government in these years to encourage a move to a settled, farming lifestyle among the Native people, which was intended to make them less dependent on a nomadic way of life. Reservations were designed to provide a specific place for Indians to settle, and Indian Agents were to provide instruction and assistance in this process. It should not be forgotten that the Native people ceded large blocks of land to the federal government that then became available for

Mrs. Grasshopper and her daughter stand in front of their wigwam in 1908. By this time most people on the Fond du Lac Reservation were living in log or frame buildings. However, Mrs. Grasshopper had lived in a traditional structure for fifty years; she also caught fish, snared rabbits, made maple syrup, harvested wild rice, and shot deer with a musket. From the collection of CCHS

A small cabin on the Fond du Lac Reservation being visited by Father Roman Homar, OSB, who in 1896 became the first resident missionary on the Reservation. The parishes had previously been served by traveling missionaries from St. John's Abbey in Collegeville. Three churches were eventually founded on the Reservation: St. Patrick's Church in 1912 in Brookston, Holy Family Church in 1889 in the Indian Village, and Sts. Mary and Joseph in 1884 at Big Lake, near Sawyer, which is the only surviving building. The Fond du Lac Catholic Indian Mission is the oldest in Minnesota and has its origins in the seventeenth-century mission activities of the Jesuits. Courtesy of the St. John's Abbey Archives

Colonel Reuben Carlton came from Onondaga, New York, in 1846 as a government blacksmith to the Ojibway. Carlton was eventually made Indian Agent at Fond du Lac, and became a strong promoter of Duluth and the surrounding region. The Minnesota legislature named the new county after Carlton in 1857. Colonel Carlton died in 1863. From the collection of CCHS

The first agricultural settlement in Carlton County was pioneered by the Finnish community along the Midway River in the early 1870s. The John Marks family established a farmstead in 1874 and were reputed to have brought the first steel plow into the area. This later photograph shows a well established farm with several frame buildings and efficient farm equipment. From the collection of EHS

Not all settlers in Carlton County were delighted to be there. Young Yella Coryell found Northern Pacific Junction a poor trade for Cedar Springs, Iowa, in 1886. From the collection of CCHS

settlement by White Americans. In the Treaty of 1854 the Lake Superior Indians ceded much of northeastern Minnesota and were granted several reservations by the government. The Fond du Lac Reservation was created out of about 100,000 acres on the south bank of the St. Louis River, in what would be Carlton and St. Louis Counties, roughly where the wintering grounds of the tribe were located.

In 1849 Minnesota became a Territory, the first step in the political process of becoming a State, and on May 23, 1857 the legislature authorized the creation of Carlton County, naming it after Colonel Reuben C. Carlton. Minnesota was made a State in 1858, but the 1860s, with the Civil War and the Sioux Uprising of 1862, were particularly hard. Not until February 18, 1870 was new legislation passed establishing Carlton County.

Thomson was one of the earliest settlements. Its importance derived from its position as a railroad junction, but it also became a lumber center and the county seat. This photograph from the mid-1880s reveals the town about ten years old. There are numerous houses, large lumber yards, and a railroad siding. A passenger train had come up the grade from Duluth and appears bound for Northern Pacific Junction. From the collection of MHS

Railroad towns and lumber towns needed boardinghouses and hotels. Mrs. Stickney's boardinghouse in Thomson was thriving in 1890. From the collection of CCHS

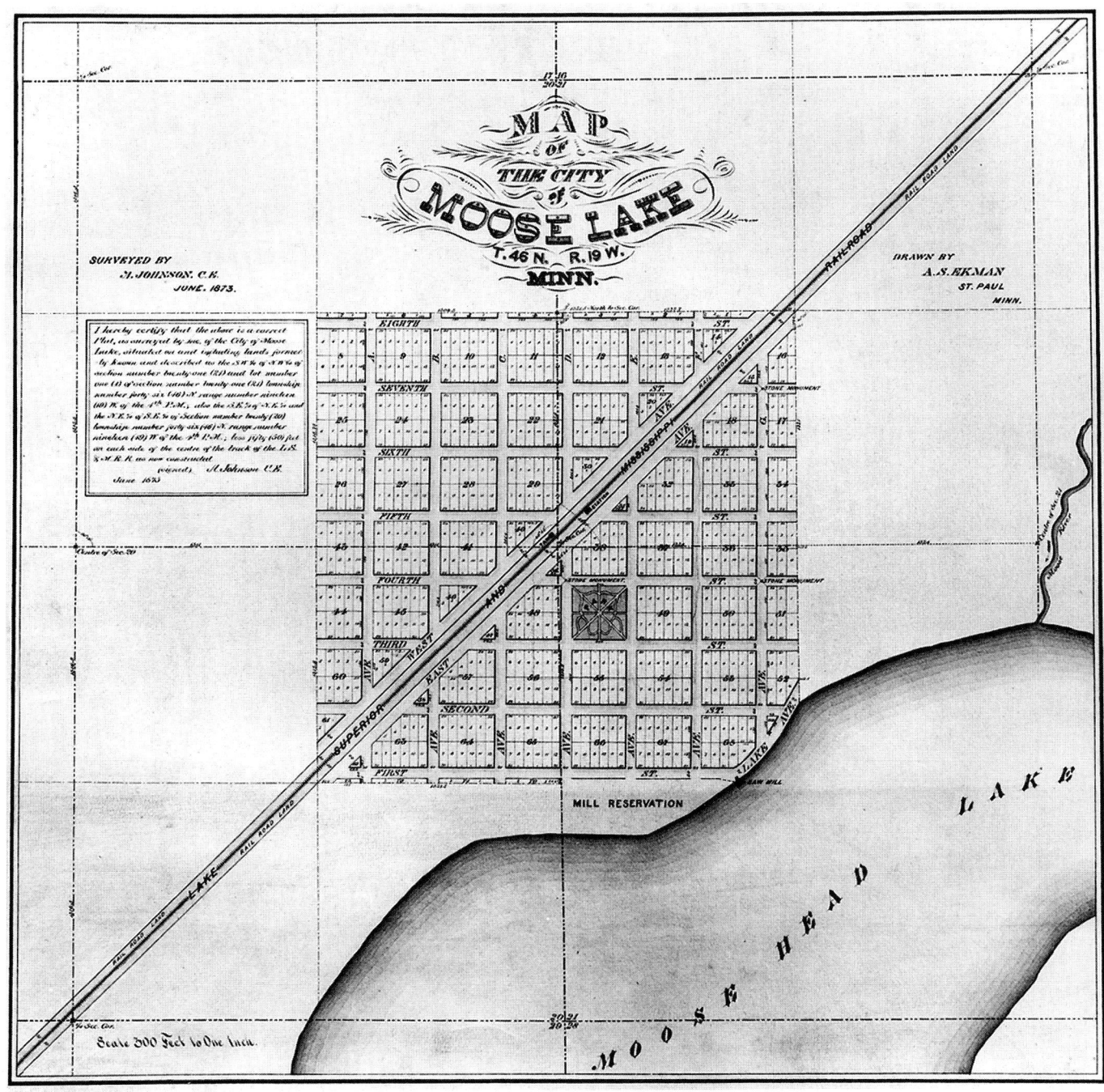

This 1873 map of Moose Lake was perhaps more a projection of what the town might become than a reflection of what existed at the time. From the collection of MHS

Named after George G. Barnum, a railroad agent, this community became both a sawmill town and a farm center. In this 1890s photograph Barnum was about twenty years old, with numerous houses and extensive railroad sidings with logs and ties waiting to be loaded. From the collection of CCHS

Mike Felgen was an early pioneer in the Barnum area who migrated to the United States from Luxemburg in 1872 and started a farm in 1879. From the collection of CCHS

Timber cruiser Dan Cameron came to Duluth in 1864, and assessed the value of the timber that could be cut in the St. Louis River valley. Cameron opened the door for the lumbermen. The woman he is shown with here may be either Grace Cameron or Emily Dunn Cameron. From the collection of CCHS

Carlton County, Minnesota 23

This photograph shows the northwest portion of Cloquet, with the C. N. Nelson and Company sawmill and yards in the upper left-hand corner. This mill became the Northern Lumber Company. Cloquet was already a thriving community. From the collection of CCHS

Wrenshall grew up in the 1880s, after the Northern Pacific Railroad built a line southeast from Carlton to Superior, Wisconsin. This frame house was built by the Rogstead family and was held to be the finest structure in the community in 1894. From the collection of CCHS

The town of Scanlon dated from the building of the Brooks-Scanlon Lumber Company along the St. Louis River. The Freeman house was one of the first homes in the village. Nelson Freeman, photographer, from the collection of CCHS

CHAPTER II

TRANSPORTATION AND THE OPENING OF CARLTON COUNTY

IT IS DIFFICULT TO IMAGINE today, with freeways and hard surfaced roads almost everywhere, how impenetrable the forest was in the nineteenth century. The St. Louis River was the main highway for Carlton County for centuries, but as a highway it was limited in what was practical to move on it. Canoes were possible, boats loaded with passengers and freight were not.

Congress attempted to provide an alternative to the St. Louis River with appropriations in 1850 to build a Military Road from Point Douglas to Lake Superior. It took ten years to complete, and all travelers who used the road complained that it was the worst they had ever experienced, but it did link the communities of southern Minnesota with the northern frontier. Mail, light cargo, and countless passengers traveled over its mud and bumps. (It took from three to six days to make the trip.) Stagecoach inns were built along the road, and the first European communities, outside the fur trade posts, had their origins in those posts. Elkton,

LEFT PAGE:

A Northern Pacific train crew pose before their small engine at a siding in Wrenshall. The fireman stands with a shovel, while the engineer, Frank Schlavine, holds the ever present oil can, used at every stop to lubricate the friction points of the locomotive. From the collection of CCHS

The Stage Hotel at Twin lakes. From the collection of CCHS

PICTURED RIGHT:
It is difficult to visualize what the Military Road must have looked like. This 1890 photograph of the dirt road between Scanlon and Carlton must approximate the old Military Road. Smith Studio photograph, from the collection of CCHS

Blackhoof, and Twin Lakes served travelers until 1870. Twin Lakes became the first county seat.

Railroads provided the best transportation alternative to rivers and dirt roads. Several railroads were chartered in Minnesota in the 1860s, including the Lake Superior and Mississippi in 1861 and the Northern Pacific in 1864. When the great financier, Jay Cooke, became involved in these projects in 1868, the money was raised and the companies were reorganized. On February 15, 1870, just outside what is now Carlton, the Northern Pacific had its beginning.

Construction also began in Duluth up the St. Louis River valley toward Thomson. The Lake Superior and Mississippi Railroad was already built to Hinckley by 1869. The summer of 1870 saw 2,000 railway men laboring furiously to lay track and to link up with the workers coming from Duluth. By the 1st of August it was done and a through train left Duluth for St. Paul the following day. At the end of the season the Northern Pacific stretched from Duluth across Carlton County all the way to Brainerd.

The Northern Pacific had a troubled history, driven to bankruptcy in 1873 and 1893, but it built Carlton County. The route of the Mississippi and Lake Superior, later absorbed into the Northern Pacific, paralleled that of the Military Road, and new towns sprang up along its right of way. Similarly, communities were built west along the Northern Pacific main line. A short line built into Knife Falls in 1879 made possible the development of the sawmill town of Cloquet, and a new grade sweeping south

Photograph taken at commencement of work on the Northern Pacific Railroad at N. P. Junction, now Carlton, Minnesota, February 15th 1870.

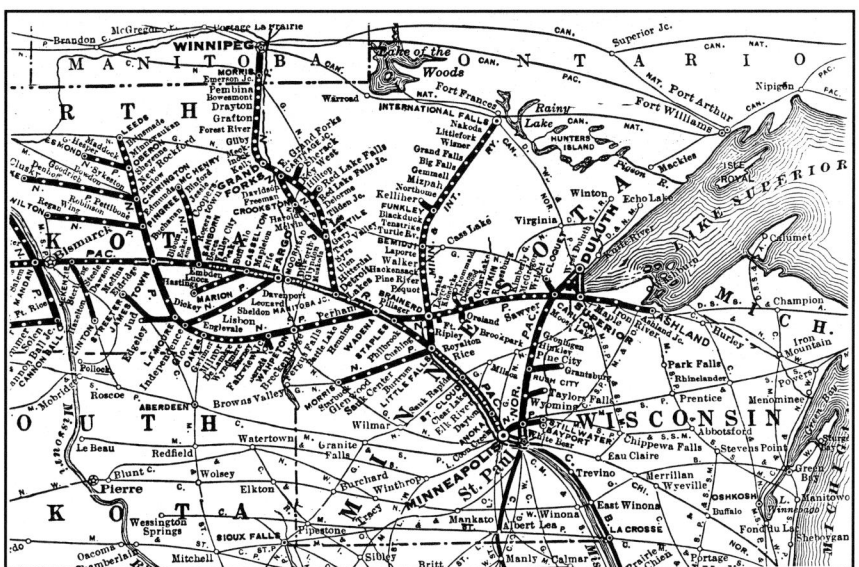

The Northern Pacific Railroad created an empire along the northern states from Minnesota west to Seattle. This turn of the century Northern Pacific map shows in bold lines the tracks that crossed the county from St. Paul to Duluth and from Duluth to the west coast. From the collection of the Lake Superior Museum of Transportation

The building of the Northern Pacific Railroad was one of the great enterprises of post-Civil War America. Work on the Northern Pacific began just west of Carlton on February 15, 1870. Building such a railroad had been proposed since the 1850s, so getting the project started was a momentous occasion. In the center, without a hat, is Dr. Thomas Foster, editor of THE DULUTH MINNESOTAN *who first called Duluth, 'The Zenith City of the Unsalted Seas.' Colonel J. B. Culver, an early mayor of Duluth, filled the first wheelbarrow. It was so cold that the ground had to be warmed by a fire in order to shovel any dirt. How much construction could take place in winter is questionable, but these were men in a hurry. From the collection of CCHS*

around the St. Louis River into Superior in 1882 facilitated the founding of Wrenshall. Within the space of just over ten years almost all the major townsites in the county came into being. The railroad, more efficiently than the Military Road, brought in settlers and supplies and carried out the fruits of their labors. Northern Pacific Junction, or Carlton as it became, was the hub of all of this action, with tracks entering

The terrain in eastern Carlton County presented challenges to railroad surveyors. This Great Northern trestle, spanning Silver Creek southeast of Carlton, shows the elaborate wooden construction used throughout the region. The largest such structure was a log trestle built across the Blackhoof River, 100 feet high and 700 feet long. From the collection of CCHS

This photograph, taken from a switch tower, shows the Carlton rail yards at their peak in the 1920s. In the foreground are the Great Northern double tracks for the huge iron ore trains bound for the ore docks in Superior. In the center left are the Northern Pacific switching yards and the main line heading west. (Minneapolis-St. Paul trains would leave the main line at a switch west of the Carlton yards.) The Northern Pacific tracks on the left were built into Wrenshall and Superior in 1882, while the straight line of tracks to the right were the old route east into Duluth through Thomson. At the bottom right of the photograph is the beginning of a switch that led tracks into Cloquet in 1879. In the center of the photograph is a "puzzle switch" to enable trains from Wrenshall either to run onto the main line or to cross the main line to the siding in front of the Northern Pacific station.

From the collection of CCHS

the town from five different directions, with depots, roundhouses, and huge switching yards.

James J. Hill's Great Northern was built through the southeast corner of the county on its way from Minneapolis to Superior in 1888. In 1896 Hill bought the bankrupt Duluth and Winnipeg Railroad that ran through Cloquet. He rebuilt this road through Carlton into Superior to the east, and he extended it west to connect with the Great Northern main line at Crookston. The last major railroad to enter the county was the Soo Line, or Minneapolis, St. Paul and Sault Ste. Marie. In 1907 construction began through Moose Lake and the southern part of the county to connect the Soo's western Minnesota lines with its yards in Superior. Moose Lake also became the junction for Soo Line tracks that were built northwest toward the Canadian border. Moose Lake became a major railroad center.

The railroads provided local freight and passenger service several times a day. They linked the small towns throughout the county, and they were also the means of contact with the wider world. As the automobile became increasingly affordable, and as road construction improved sufficiently to permit trucks to provide reliable service, the railroads began to face competition.

Two towermen stand on the landing of the Northern Pacific switch tower in Carlton in 1922. From their elevated position they could see the length of the Carlton yards and at the appropriate moment throw the switches that would direct freight trains into the sidings, passenger trains along the station platform, and express trains straight through on the main line. From the collection of CCHS

The Brooks-Scanlon Lumber Company ran a logging railroad, the Minnesota and North Wisconsin, to bring in logs from its operations north of Cloquet. Five locomotives can be seen in this photograph, but the company had four more in the woods. Beyond the round house roof can be seen the burner for the company's Scanlon sawmill. From the collection of CCHS

Carlton County, Minnesota ❧ 31

The train depot played a varied role in the life of turn-of-the-century communities. Outings or picnics or family reunions might well start at the depot where a special car would be arranged for the occasion, as seems to be the case at this Barnum depot at the turn of the century. The depot with its telegraph office was the town communication center. Freight and agricultural produce was generally shipped by train, but special goods were sent through the express office that would also be located at the depot. From the collection of CCHS

PICTURED BELOW:

The station master of the Soo Line depot at Kettle River sits at his desk, while the dray line operator, Charles Korhonen, on the right stands ready to make his deliveries. From the collection of CCHS

A group of immigrant women who have recently arrived from Sweden stand in front of the Northern Pacific depot at Atkinson. In the background is the Bethel Swedish Lutheran Church, and on the platform stands a milk can, waiting for the "milk" train. From the collection of CCHS

PICTURED TOP TO BOTTOM:

(1) The Ziebler Hotel was the first in Barnum built for train crews and traveling salesmen. Mrs. Ziebler is shown on the right, with her staff. From the collection of CCHS

(2) The Soo Line depot in Moose Lake was one of the larger stations in the county. The tracks have been taken up recently, but the depot survived the 1918 fire and has been restored and serves as a museum for the Moose Lake Area Historical Society. Maintenance of the tracks required regular attention, and here a section crew is shown at work keeping the rails level. From the collection of MLAHS

(3) It was hoped that the Soo Restaurant in Moose Lake would exploit railroad traffic around the depot. From the collection of MLAHS

Northern Pacific track crews are shown here in 1883 putting in a spur from their main line to a sawmill. The size of the crew gives some suggestion of the large number of people employed by the railroads in these years. From the collection of MLAHS

Track is being laid in the lumber yard of one of the Cloquet sawmills in the early 1900s. The men with large hammers drove the spikes into the ties in order to hold the rails in place. The men with long bars kept the rails aligned as they were being spiked to the ties. These new tracks are resting on the bare ground. Later gravel or crushed rock, termed ballast, would be poured around the ties to form a secure bed and the tracks would be leveled. From the collection of CCHS

The weight and pounding of the locomotives created maintenance problems that led to regular derailments and wrecks. Large railroad centers had steam cranes and experienced crews ready to speed to the scene of a train wreck in order to salvage the equipment, fix the track, and get the traffic moving as quickly as possible. This Great Northern iron ore train, west of Cloquet in 1909, was badly wrecked, as the twisted cars and rails suggest. However, the railroad was fortunate to have double track which allowed the crane to come alongside to do its work. Smith Studio photograph, from the collection of CCHS

PICTURED ABOVE:

Of the several logging railroads in the county, the sole survivor is the Duluth and Northeastern Railroad. Although the railroad had several roles, a major function is shown here, where a locomotive pulls a trainload of logs across the St. Louis River onto Dunlap Island on its way to the sawmills in Cloquet. Smith Studio photograph, from the collection of CCHS

The awkward and fragile looking "International" automobile, shown here with Judge F. A. Watkins of Carlton and his family in 1909, would hardly seem a threat to the booming world that the Northern Pacific and the Great Northern had created. But even with its folding top, puncture-proof tires, bulb horn, kerosene head lamps, and right-hand drive, this was the future of transportation in both Carlton County and America. From the collection of CCHS

Good road building became a necessity with the development of the automobile. Here, in the 1930s, concrete was being poured to make the highway at the St. Louis River bridge at Scanlon. Nelson Freeman, photographer, from the collection of CCHS

CHAPTER III

THE WORLD OF FARMING

Farming was the great American dream of the nineteenth century. It was at the heart of Jeffersonianism and Jacksonianism, and it was also the basis of the Homestead Act in 1862. It was the objective of much of the government's Indian policy, and it was the hope of millions of European immigrants. Farming was certainly the driving force of early settlement in Carlton County.

It can be said that the Ojibway at Fond du Lac were the first farmers, harvesting wild rice and wild fruit, growing corn, and producing maple sugar. European style farming was introduced on a small scale at the stagecoach stops, where both vegetables and fodder were grown at the stations. However, the Finnish settlers who started homesteads along the Midway River in 1873 were the first systematic farmers. They raised grain crops and by 1878 built a gristmill on the property of Erick Palki. By the

LEFT PAGE:

This is a classic picture of the rural American dream of the nineteenth century. Here at the turn of the century is a Moose Lake area family taking in an oat crop by hand. Oats are cut with a traditional scythe, while a wooden rake is used to gather the oats into bunches that are then shocked, or stooked, into bundles to dry. While the girl and the baby look at the camera, the horse seems to understand that this crop of oats is being prepared for him. From the collection of MLAHS

Here a Fond du Lac Ojibway family is processing wild rice, or "manomin." This aquatic grass grew in abundance in shallow water. In August and September the plants would be harvested by shaking the ripe kernels into a canoe. The kernels were then dried and the husks removed, either by walking on the kernels with soft moccasins or by pounding gently with staffs, as shown here. The finished rice provided a staple food. Traditional birchbark baskets can be seen at the bottom of the photograph. From the collection of CCHS

early twentieth century the Midway River, or Esko area, became famous for its dairy production.

Farming was also initiated in the little settlements that grew up along the Lake Superior and Mississippi Railroad tracks angling northeast through the county. Here too cereal crops and vegetables were produced and shipped to markets in Duluth and St. Paul on the railroad. Indeed, the railroads encouraged agricultural settlement by establishing a model farm at Mahtowa.

The soil and climate of northern Minnesota did not allow farmers of Carlton County to compete successfully with wheat farmers in other parts of the American west. This problem was perceived by Hans Carl Hanson, the Barnum banker. In 1904 Hanson bought a creamery in Barnum and began to encourage farmers to improve the quality of the milk and eggs they sold, first through quality control procedures and then through improved strains of purebred dairy cattle and laying hens. By the 1920s

The Augustus Clemons homestead was settled north of Cloquet in 1895. By 1906 the farm was quite well developed. From the collection of CCHS

Hanson and others had created something of an economic miracle. As a result of all of these efforts, farm income from creameries rose from $27,057 in 1909 to $104,417 in 1918, while income from egg sales rose from $3,000 in 1909 to $41,274 in 1919. The spread of Cooperative societies in other parts of the county also contributed to improved farm marketing and incomes. This thriving farm community in the county can be seen in the steadily increasing population from 1880 to 1940. Even during the decades following the Great 1918 Fire, when the population of Cloquet actually fell, the rural population of Carlton County increased.

Converting cut-over forest land to farm land was a laborious process. This moveable crane, operating near Wrenshall, piled the stumps for burning. Earlier the stumps would have been broken loose with dynamite, or in some cases blown up. E. Ayres, photographer, from the collection of CCHS

While most early farms in the county were modest in size, there were several very large farms. This farm was owned by the Watkins family south of Carlton near Lake Venoah. This early 1900s photograph shows at least six large farm buildings, a large frame house at the left (probably for the Watkins family), and a story-and-a-half log house at the right (probably for the hired workers). All of the people and teams of horses may have been at the farm for a special occasion, but the numerous farm animals visible are indicative of the variety of livestock kept on the farm. Surely this was success in nineteenth-century America. From the collection of CCHS

PICTURED BELOW:
The Edward and Hannah Wold farm was started in 1892, southwest of Moose Lake. Their children, Lindy and Lee, are shown here sitting on a wagon loaded with slab wood from a sawmill on the Moose River. The wagon is drawn by a team of two oxen, weighing about a ton each. The farm was destroyed by the 1918 fires. From the collection of MLAHS

Reverend Abraham Mallinen settled with his family north of Thompson in 1883. The first licensed minister in Thomson, he served as pastor of the Apostolic Lutheran Church of Esko when it was organized. Pastor Mallinen confirmed the first class of children in the area. He is shown here on his farm in 1899. From the collection of the EHS

"Thou shalt not plow with an ox and an ass together." Deuteronomy, 22:10. Joseph Kubat of Cromwell seems confident that this prohibition does not apply to his horse. The horse looks uncertain. From the collection of CCHS

Horses were the main source of both power and transportation in the pre-combustion engine rural world. The Carlton Horse Market on the Webbeking farm was the automobile dealership of its day. The size of the crowd at this 1914 auction gives some indication of the central place held by horses in the life of the county. From the collection of CCHS

PICTURED BELOW:
The local grain elevator bought such cereal crops as were grown in the county and also sold seeds to local farmers. The Carlton elevator owner Bob Roley is shown here in 1925 with George LaVoi and an unidentified woman clerk. From the collection of CCHS

The Carlton Feed and Livery stable performed a function needed in every town—stabling horses, renting them, and selling hay and fodder. This particular business also traded horses. In this photograph, the owner, Ed Armstrong, sits in the buggy, while his assistants hold horses available for rent. Charlie Goman sits on the Duluth Brewing and Malting Company wagon in front of their office.
From the collection of CCHS

44 ❧ Reflections Of Our Past

Cereal crops began with seeding, and here Andrew Mattson of Pleasant Valley is shown using a small machine which spreads in front of him an even distribution of seeds as he turns the crank at the side of the contraption and walks forward at a steady pace. This picture was taken in the 1920s. From the collection of CCHS

John Habhegger is shown here cutting grain on the Sprecker farm near Wrenshall with a team of three horses pulling a mower. The grain is left in swaths on the ground by the mower and will then have to be bundled together in shocks to dry. T. J. Streeter, photographer, From the collection of CCHS

The history of American agriculture has been the story of the steady mechanization of the agricultural process. Steam traction engines made their appearance in the 1880s and by the early twentieth century gasoline powered tractors arrived. This huge gasoline powered tractor is shown pulling a Rumley Ideal Thresher on the William Erickson farm near Blackhoof in 1915. It was the wave of the future. From the collection of CCHS

Machinery Day in Barnum, 1902, was the occasion for local farmers to collect their newly purchased farm equipment—mostly hay rakes and mowers. This is a dramatic illustration of the process of mechanization in Carlton County. From the collection of CCHS

By the early twentieth century dairy farming emerged as the most profitable farm enterprise in the Carlton County area. Hans Carl Hanson, the Barnum banker, became the leader in a program to improve the quality of dairy products and to introduce purebred Guernsey cattle into the local herds. Here is a Guernsey, "Bessie" by name, from a Scanlon area farm in the early 1900s. Nelson Freeman, photographer, from the collection of CCHS

The Barnum Creamery, purchased by H. C. Hanson in 1904, became the center of improved dairy production in the county. Cans of milk are being delivered by farmers to the creamery for processing. From the collection of CCHS

Large scale creamery operations were essentially an industrial process. Milk was separated from cream, pasteurized, and bottled for sale. Butter, buttermilk, and various kinds of cheeses were also made. A creamery was an essential establishment in every farm service center. Russell Livingston, Emil Lampinen, John Wournos, Charles Korhonen, and the daughter of John Wournos, stand on the gleaming wet floors before their machinery in the Kettle River Creamery in 1924. From the collection of CCHS

The John G. Carlson family from the Blackhoof area made maple syrup in 1909, as the Ojibway had done before them. From the collection of CCHS

Local cucumbers had a market in 1918 at the Moose Lake Pickle Factory. From the collection of MLAHS

CLOVER DALE COLONY

Wright, Carlton County, Minn.

One of the many healthful sections of America, located in one of the most progressive States in the Union. Contiguous to Duluth, the second largest shipping port on the Great Lakes, and to the consuming markets of the Minnesota iron and lumber regions and the Twin Cities of St. Paul and Minneapolis. Well watered by small streams and many pretty lakes; traversed by transcontinental railway lines. One of the best timbered sections in the state, with prairie openings and meadow land. Climate, soil, grasses, raw material and markets greatly favor the farmers, stock raisers, dairymen and manufacturers.

WE ARE THE PEOPLE

Our demands should be respected.

Give us good homes, plenty to eat, and comfortable clothes.

Give us education, training, and good society.

Give us Clover Dale Land Company land.

We are entitled to the best and should have it.

We Are to Inherit the Earth

Prepare us for this great responsibility by giving us what we demand, and we will become honest, industrious, upright citizens, proud of our ancestry and loyal to our country.

No portion of America offers greater opportunities for the intelligent home seeker than does Aitkin and Carlton counties today, and nowhere can good lands be secured at as low rates. The apparent difficulty of getting products to market will inevitably be swept away as soon as the supplies are ready for shipment. There is no reason why this entire section should not in a few years become the ideal stock, dairy and truck farm region of America. And it surely will. For further information write

CLOVER DALE LAND COMPANY

PETER JOHNSON, Field Manager, Wright, Carlton Co., Minn.

Agricultural land was actively promoted at the turn of the century. This advertisement literally promises the "Earth" to those willing to purchase land in the Clover Dale Colony in western Carlton County. The American dream! From the collection of CCHS

CHAPTER IV

THE WHEELS OF INDUSTRY

LEFT PAGE:

The mighty eastern white pine was at the heart of the lumber industry in Carlton County. Here white pine logs, several feet in diameter, are being loaded onto railroad bogies. Even with the advent of logging railroads, which enabled cutting and swamping operations to continue into the summer, horses were used for power to get the logs to the track and onto the train. From the collection of CCHS

Carlton County has an economic history that is tied to both agriculture and industry. The key industries have been those related to forest enterprises, although there have been others of considerable significance also. This fact has given the history of the county a distinctive richness and complexity.

Logging operations and sawmills were the earliest industrial enterprises in the county. The first logging took place along the Nemadji River in the 1850s, as sawmills in Superior and Duluth cut white pine in that rich river valley. Early logging on the Kettle River and its tributaries sent timber down the St. Croix River to Stillwater. The first sawmills in Carlton County were located at Thomson as soon as it was possible to ship lumber out by train. The most successful of the first three Thomson mills was that of Andreas M. Miller, who moved his operations from Duluth to the mouth of the Midway River in 1871. J. M. Paine moved his sawmill from Duluth to Northern Pacific Junction. Other mills in the

Traditional logging operations were confined to winter so that the heavy logs could be skidded on the snow and then loaded onto sleds which were drawn by horses along iced roads in the woods, as shown in this photograph. This remained a practical way of cutting timber well into the twentieth century, but the logging railroads began to change things. In the meantime, great pride was taken in piling as many logs as possible on the sleds in order to surpass the work of others in the logging camp. From the collection of CCHS

1870s were built in Moose Lake, Barnum, and Mahtowa. Logging operations and small sawmills followed the Northern Pacific main line west to Cromwell and Wright in the 1880s, and the Fond du Lac Reservation was opened to cutting in 1904. By the early twentieth century, extensive logging was also done near Automba and Kettle River.

The construction in 1879 of railroad tracks north from Northern Pacific Junction to Knife Falls, made it possible for sawmills to be built above the Knife Falls. The Knife Falls Lumber Company was taken over by Frederick Weyerhaeuser and George S. Shaw in 1883 and reorganized as the Renwick, Shaw and Crosset Company and in 1886 as the Cloquet Lumber Company. C. N. Nelson and company built a sawmill in 1880, across from Dunlap Island. In 1895 the Weyerhaeuser group were able to purchase Nelson's holdings, which were

Camps would be built in the woods in the autumn to make facilities for the lumberjacks, teamsters, cooks, blacksmiths, clerks, and others. Often as many as one hundred men would arrive with the first snows and begin cutting trees. These men were working in the Clark and Jackson Camp near Wrenshall in 1899. The majestic white pines can be seen quite close to the buildings, although the two lumberjacks holding a crosscut saw to the tree at the left are doing so for the benefit of the photographer, no doubt. There are four teams of horses, that would have been as important as the men. The several pigs at the right would make their contribution in the dining hall. From the collection of CCHS

re-named the Northern Lumber Company. The Barnum lumberman, Samuel S. Johnson, moved his mill to Cloquet in 1894 and built the Johnson-Wentworth Company. The Weyerhaeuser associates were given the opportunity to buy this mill in 1902. By the early twentieth century Cloquet emerged as the center of the Weyerhaeuser forest industries in Minnesota.

Logging and sawmills on this enormous scale generated a variety of allied industries. The most conspicuous at the time were the logging railroads, first introduced in the county in the 1880s by J. M. Paine and Company. In the 1890s the Nelson Lumber Company built the Mesabe Southern Railway and the Cloquet Lumber Company started the Duluth and Northeastern Railroad, which still survives. There were also a variety of planing mills, power plants, barns and stables, shops, foundries, boom companies, camp suppliers, company stores, and marketing firms. These enterprises employed hundreds of people, from pattern makers and foundry men to office managers and log scalers. The Northwest Paper Company was founded in 1898 as a means of using spruce and pine unsuitable for saw logs, as were the box factory and the clothespin-match factory. Control of the market for logs by the Cloquet sawmills encouraged the formation of the Brooks-Scanlon Lumber Company in 1901 at what became the town of Scanlon.

Two other heavy industries, unrelated to the wood products, flourished in the Carlton County. The first was brick manufacturing, which started along the Northern Pacific tracks near the Wisconsin border at Barker. Fred J. Habhegger moved his operations to Wrenshall in 1887 and built a new brick plant and kiln there. This was the first of three brick plants that produced an estimated 600,000,000 bricks, and provided the building materials for many of the

It has been said that the cooks were the most important men in the camps. If the food was good, the men were happy and willing to work. If the food was bad, the men drifted away to work in other camps, leaving the foreman hard pressed to cut his assigned volume of timber. This 1898 camp kitchen, near Carlton, looks like a smart operation. From the collection of CCHS

Bunkhouse facilities were fairly modest in the logging camps. Warmth and cleanliness, rather than comfort or privacy, were its strengths. From the collection of CCHS

brick buildings in northeastern Minnesota. The second major industry was the production of hydroelectric power. Jay Cooke obtained the riparian rights to the lower St. Louis River. Before he died in 1905 he set in motion the building of a dam at the falls at Thomson, together with a canal that would draw the river water east to turbines at the river level, almost three miles from the dam. It was one of the largest engineering projects in the United States at the time.

The blacksmith was a key figure in the economy of the early logging camps. Except for the axes, saw blades, and harnesses for the horses, the blacksmith made much of the equipment used in a logging camp—most notably the skidding gear, the loading machinery, the sleds for logs, and the water tanks for icing the roads. Of course, the blacksmith also put shoes on horses. Nelson Freeman, photographer, from the collection of CCHS

The timber cut in the winter was floated down stream to the mills in the spring. Driving the logs in the rivers was a specialized skill. In this picture, taken about 1900, the men have chained the logs together to form a raft. In order to keep their footing on the wet logs, they would wear boots with spiked, or calked, soles. Several of the men are carrying long pikes to push the logs, while others have shorter handled peaveys which also have cant hooks with which they can twist the logs.

From the collection of CCHS

Some streams did not have enough water to float the logs. This crisis could be met by building temporary driving dams that would raise the water level sufficiently to float the logs and hopefully get them into deeper water. Here are driving dams along the St. Louis River, or one of its tributaries, in 1918. Stranded timber can be seen piled along the banks of the river and in the mud. From the collection of CCHS

The destination of all of these logs was the sawmill. This early photograph shows the crew of the Andreas Miller Lumber Company in Thomson, on the Midway River. Miller moved his sawmill from Duluth to Thomson in 1870 to take advantage of the new railroad. The rivers gave him access to previously untapped timberlands and the railroad opened up national markets. Miller made a fortune.

From the collection of EHS

A modest steam traction engine allowed small portable sawmills to spring up near a stand of trees. Such an operation might lack a planing mill and drying yard, but it could certainly provide rough lumber for farm buildings. This photograph shows Albert Gray and his crew running a portable sawmill near Moose Lake in April 1919. No doubt rough lumber was much in demand after the 1918 fire.

From the collection of MLAHS

This Carlson sawmill in Blackhoof township is a good example of a mid-sized mill. The belts in the center of the picture converted the power from a steam engine to the wheels that drove the machinery in the mill. The sawyer, the key man in running a mill, stands with his hand on the lever that moved the carriage holding the log to be cut. G. N. Forslund, photographer, from the collection of CCHS

The Johnson-Wentworth Company sawmill, constructed in 1894, was the largest single sawmill in the United States. The mill had three separate saws and had a capacity to produce between seventy and eighty million board feet of lumber a year. The dam in the foreground of the picture created a "hot" pond in which logs could be kept floating until they were drawn up into the mill on a "bull chain," the diagonal structure entering the mill building on the second floor. The logs were moved up the chain and then rolled onto a carriage for one of the three saws. Sawdust and scraps would be consumed in the burner on the left. From the collection of CCHS

The large lumber companies in Cloquet required countless skilled tradesmen to keep their complex machinery running. Here, in 1930, a large Northern Lumber Company bandsaw is being sharpened with very specialized equipment by Chris Berg, saw filer. From the collection of MHS

Carlton County, Minnesota ❦ 57

The enormous production of the big mills in Cloquet resulted in rows of this fresh cut lumber piled in huge stacks to be dried. It was this lumber, drying in the sun, that generated the smell of pine that Walter O'Meara remembered as epitomizing Cloquet.

From the collection of CCHS

Nineteenth-century company stores had advantages and disadvantages in the form of credit and a lack of independence. This Sauntry and Cain store near Barnum, shown here in 1911, looked well stocked and flourishing. From the collection of CCHS

PICTURED MID-LEFT:

The lumber companies in Cloquet also had company stores, houses, and boardinghouses. This large building was the Northern Lumber Company boardinghouse, shown at the turn of the century. The proprietor was Louis Leimer, and both his staff of cooks and housekeepers and his customers can be seen here on the porch. Are the youngsters guests, or neighbor children? From the collection of CCHS

PICTURED BOTTOM LEFT:

Founded in 1898 by the lumber companies in Cloquet to exploit the trees that could not be used for saw logs, the Northwest Paper Company outlived its parents. The plant, shown here from the north side of the St. Louis River, was not damaged by the 1918 fire. Clearly visible here is the dam that provided electrical power for the mill. An early dam had driven the grinders to make mechanical pulp. From the collection of CCHS

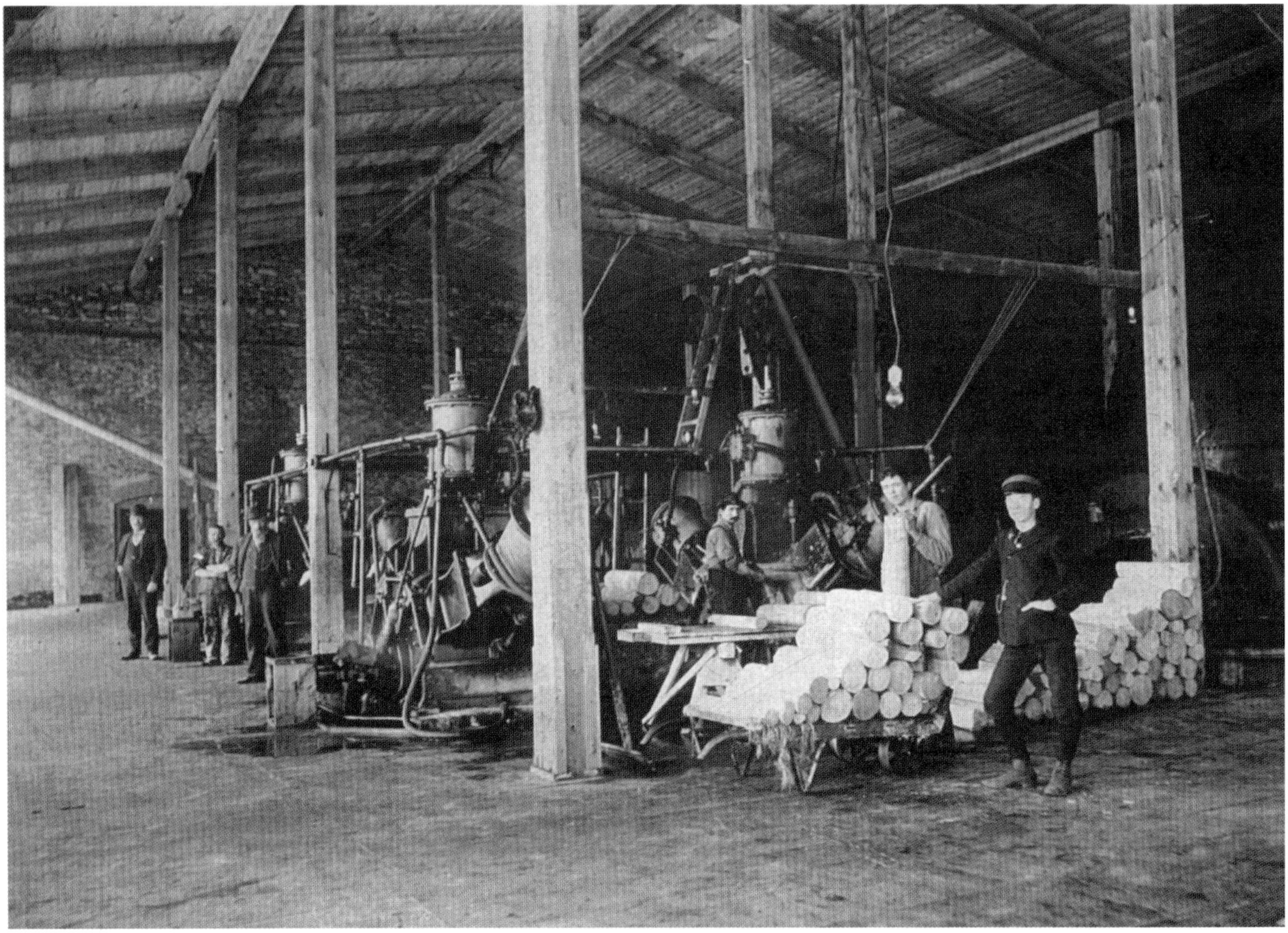

This photograph shows the groundwood pulp mill in 1899, the year Northwest Paper went into production. This mill produced the pulp to manufacture newsprint, and in April THE PINE KNOT was printed with paper from the first successful run. From the collection of CCHS

Cloquet was the site of the Berst (later Berst-Forster-Dixfield) match mill in 1905. This picture shows the workers on a picnic the following year, 1906. From the collection of CCHS

The great thirty-eight-foot dam at Thomson, built between 1905 and 1907, created a reservoir holding 130 million cubic feet of water. This water traveled several miles through a canal and underground pipes, dropping 374 feet to a generating station farther downriver. The construction of the Thomson dam and the generating facilities was one of the great engineering projects of its day. Nelson Freeman, photographer, from the collection of CCHS

PICTURED BELOW:
These children are visiting the mechanical room at the Thomson dam. The instrument panel seen here in the dam itself controlled the level of water in the reservoir and the volume of water flowing through the dalles of the St. Louis River. Nelson Freeman, photographer, from the collection of CCHS

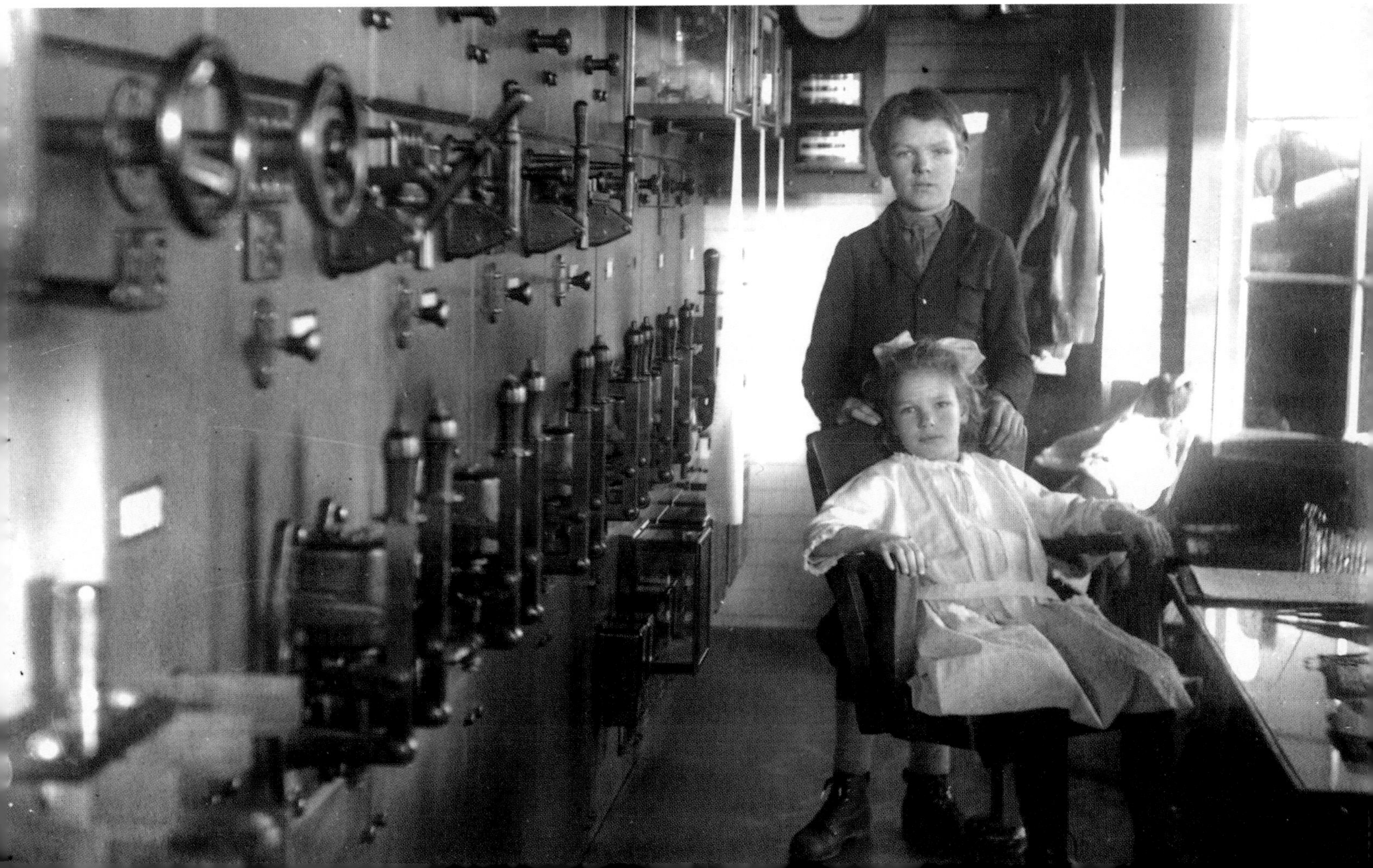

The demand for electricity was so great in the early twentieth century that eventually hydro-electric power was generated on the St. Louis River from two dams in Cloquet, one in Scanlon, and one at Fond du Lac, as well as through the Thomson dam. This photograph shows the construction of the great curved dam at Fond du Lac, built in 1924. It was the last built in the county and one of the largest in the state—500 feet long and 80 feet high. The north side is in St. Louis County and the south side in Carlton County. Courtesy of Minnesota Power

Construction was started in Cloquet in 1921 to build the Wood Conversion Company which would produce Balsam-Wool, a wood fiber insulation, and Nu-Wood, a composition board. The promotion of these new and innovative products took some imagination. These two elves, standing in front of the main office, helped to make the product famous. From the collection of CCHS

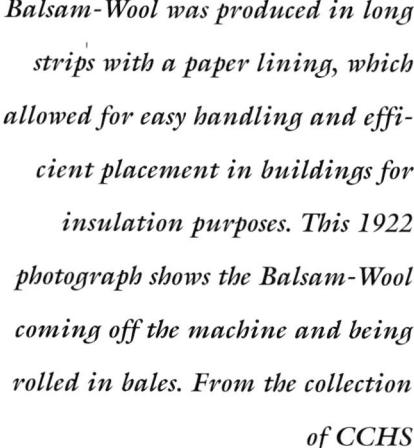

Balsam-Wool was produced in long strips with a paper lining, which allowed for easy handling and efficient placement in buildings for insulation purposes. This 1922 photograph shows the Balsam-Wool coming off the machine and being rolled in bales. From the collection of CCHS

Brick making also took place on a smaller scale in Barnum and Moose Lake. During the mid-1920s the Moose Lake Tile and Pottery Company employed thirty people. *From the collection of MLAHS*

The Habhegger brick plant was the first of three brick factories in Wrenshall. This photograph, taken in 1899, shows the raw bricks stacked carefully with spaces in between them to allow heat to bake all of the bricks in the kiln. From the collection of CCHS

Carlton County, Minnesota ※ 63

CHAPTER V

TOWNS AND SETTLEMENTS

LEFT PAGE:

Here is the 1903 graduating class of Barnum High School. Seated were Clara Hecker, Mr. Brophy (principal), Louise Kreiger, and Lorraine Balton; standing were Pearl Skelton, Mayme Lee, Luella Goodell, Ray Addington, Minnie Siemer, and Hannah Johnson. George G. Barnum gave a twenty dollar gold piece to each graduate. Octavie Morneau, photographer, from the collection of CCHS

Town life in Carlton County was determined by railroads and economics. In 1870 Thomson become a rail junction, and as result a sawmill center, the market for the Midway River settlement, and the county seat. It had a general store, a hotel, a school, a church, and a doctor. However, subsequent railroad construction during the next decade expanded out of Northern Pacific Junction, and the newer settlement became the rail hub. In 1889 the county seat was moved to Northern Pacific Junction, which changed its name to "Carlton." By 1900 Carlton had five stores, four hotels, eight saloons, several churches, a woman doctor, a bank, and a newspaper.

Towns grew up very quickly along the railroad south to St. Paul. Moose Lake had its origins in the old stage stop of Elkton, but the building of the railroad brought in many more people and by 1872 it had several sawmills, company stores, a general store, two hotels, and a saloon. In 1880 Moose Lake township was the largest in the county, with 613

This Moose Lake building was Knutilas's Store at the turn of the century. It appears to have sold general merchandise. Bolts of cloth, soap, pickles, oars, and shovels can be identified on the display, although we might assume that the man holding two fish caught them himself. The store also served as the Post Office, and the two women seen in the upper window are thought to be telephone operators. Fom the collection of MLAHS

people. By 1910, following the building of the Soo Line through Moose Lake, the population of the town itself reached 520. Barnum and Mahtowa were both stops along the Northern Pacific tracks, but the railroad itself made possible the early sawmills. Barnum was incorporated in 1889, and during that decade had acquired several stores and hotels and a school. Barnum also became a major farm center, as the sawmills closed down. Other towns along the Northern Pacific line were Iverson, Sawyer, Cromwell, and Wright.

The eastern and far western towns in the county also developed through railroad facilities. When the Northern Pacific extended track to Superior south of the St. Louis River valley in 1881–1882 it opened up a new area that had been cut over by lumbermen. Wrenshall became a base

John and Irene Lindmark (on the right), were Moose Lake's first druggists. From the collection of MLAHS

66 ❧ Reflections Of Our Past

for many of the farmers in this area. Farther south, Holyoke was built along the Great Northern tracks from Minneapolis to Superior in 1888. The last railroad to build through the county was the Soo Line, and helped develop Moose Lake, Kettle River, and Automba. Settlers came to this region as early as the 1870s and the villages of Salo and Automba had post offices as early as 1903.

In 1907 sporting gents could refresh themselves in H. K. Lower's bar in Moose Lake. A benign Lower stands to the right, while Haugbert Pederson behind the gleaming bar is ready to draw a schooner of beer for his thirsty customers. From the collection of MLAHS

Even Esko and Scanlon had railroad connections. Named after Alexander Esko, a railroad land agent, this community had its origins in the Midway River settlement of the 1870s, but the cluster of houses that constituted the village grew up along the short-lived Duluth and Winnipeg Railroad. Esko became a major farm service center after roads were built to Cloquet and Duluth. The village of Scanlon grew up around the Brooks-Scanlon Lumber Company in 1901. It became a thriving town with a post office, a town hall, schools, a volunteer fire department,

Mr. Culver of Carlton provided the first mail delivery service in the Blackhoof region. From the collection of CCHS

Carlton County, Minnesota ❧ 67

and numerous churches, and it even survived the departure of the sawmill in 1909. The Northern Pacific tracks ran past Scanlon, but they were in place well before the town was settled.

Cloquet was the largest city in Carlton County, and it was tied to the building of Northern Pacific tracks into Knife Falls in 1879, making possible the operation of several sawmills. The mills were strung out along the river with settlements clustered around them named after the owners—"Shaw town," "Nelson town," and "Johnson town." In 1884 they were incorporated into the village of Cloquet, and in 1904, with a population of over 3,000, Cloquet became a city. There was a volunteer fire department by 1888, a professional department by 1902, and a police department by 1907. By the early twentieth century there were five hotels, a number of boardinghouses, eleven merchants, a variety of specialty shops. In 1885 THE PINE KNOT was founded, in 1888 the first of several banks and investment companies, two telephone companies, and a power company. Schools were started in 1881 and by 1905 there was a new high school and several grade schools. The first church in the town

The mail was delivered on foot in Cloquet. This 1916 photograph shows William Boyer, Joe Franklin, Julius Samuelson, and Elton Sanborn ready to begin their routes. From the collection of CCHS

was the Catholic Church of the Holy Names of Jesus and Mary, built in 1882 (which became Our Lady of the Sacred Heart in 1902), and it was followed the next year by the founding of the Presbyterian Church. A large number of churches, many with an ethnic orientation, were built over the next several decades. The population, which had reached 7,031 in the 1910 census, was estimated to be between eight and nine thousand in 1918.

A printer was essential in every community. This was Willie Newman's printing shop in Mahtowa in 1910. Willie can be seen leaning against one of his type cases, while on the other side of the room is a small press and a paper cutter. From the collection of CCHS

Julius B. Baumann, the register of deeds, stands in his office in the court house with his clerks, Lotti Olson Michaelson, Ida Carlson and Winona Watkins. From the collection of CCHS

S. A. Jacobson owned the Carlton Bank, and he is shown here with one of his clerks. In 1910 he also bought the bank in Moose Lake.
From the collection of MLAHS

Gus Moser's Meat Market in Carlton had sausages hanging on the wall, fresh cuts of meat on the counter, and chops and steaks cooling on a slab of marble, no doubt. Was there sawdust on the floor?
From the collection of CCHS

One of the leading automobile dealerships in the county was the Carlton Motor Company, a large prosperous-looking brick structure, with gas pumps on the street for "curb service." Standing with her staff in this 1920s photograph is Clara Holmes, the owner. Kuhn of Stillwater, photographer, from the collection of CCHS

The old fashioned barber shop was a men's institution for which no contemporary counterpart exists. This 1910 Cloquet tonsorial emporium is a classic. The two hair dressers stand by their chairs, with suitable ointments and exotic perfumes on the marble shelf before the mirror. On the opposite wall is a rack holding the distinctive shaving mugs of regular customers. A gentleman would be shaved by his barber, but perhaps only once or twice a week. In front of the chairs is a spittoon for the patron's convenience. Elaborate gas lamps illuminate the room, but where are the copies of the POLICE GAZETTE? From the collection of CCHS

There were several kinds of exclusively women's shops also, of which this millinery store is a good example. A fashion conscious lady would not simply buy a new hat, but would have one made to match her other garments. This photograph shows Myrt Johnson with a customer in the East End Hat and Art Shoppe in Cloquet in the 1930s. Courtesy of Gene Cary and Betty Anne Hebert

A beer wagon has just made a delivery of supplies to the Mortensen Saloon in Scanlon. Meals were also available at the "Lumber Jacks Restaurant." From the collection of CCHS

By 1904 Scanlon had its own volunteer fire department. Here is a pumper and hose reel, surrounded by a suitably uniformed volunteer fire brigade. From the collection of CCHS

Every community, no matter how small, created a school system and took pride in the school's activities. Here sits the Cloquet High School graduating class of 1898. Their teacher, Miss B. Johnson of Duluth, and a graduate of the University of Michigan, stands against the blackboard. From the collection of CCHS

In a community made up of diverse ethnic societies, language groups, and cultural orientation, educational systems were expected to engender a sense of American national identity, if not patriotism. These Washington School boys in Cloquet constituted a drill team. They were equipped with wooden rifles and dressed in uniforms reminiscent of the Spanish-American War soldiers. Included in their number were Ojibway boys from the Fond du Lac Reservation. From the collection of CCHS

This group of children attended the Indian Day School near the Holy Family Church in the Indian Village west of Cloquet. The school was a log building covered with wooden siding. From the collection of the St. John's Abbey Archives

Our Lady of the Sacred Heart Catholic Church provided parochial education in Cloquet up to grade eight. This photograph shows the 1918 graduating eighth grade class. Students desiring high school education in Cloquet could continue in the public school system. From the collection of CCHS

A central cultural institution in larger towns was the public library. Moose Lake, Barnum, Carlton, and Cloquet all had libraries. Sometime in the 1920s, these children sit listening to the librarian in the Cloquet library, perhaps to a story. This building, the Shaw Memorial Library, is now the home of the Carlton County Historical Society. From the collection of CCHS

Are not these charming Wrenshall Elementary School children, with their teacher, J. H. Eschelman, an American idyl? Hoods, scarfs, capes, mufflers, knee-britches, mackinaws, Eton collars, fur hats, broad-brimmed hats—who could top this? H. A. Stimson, photographer, from the collection of CCHS

Not everything was idyllic, however. The Carlton School burned in 1914. Such calamities were not uncommon before central heating. A. Rue, photographer, from the collection of CCHS

At a time of very active church participation, many children went to Sunday School, and for many first- or second-generation immigrant children the church was also the center of their ethnic cultural orientation. This smartly dressed group of young people, participants in the first Sunday School in Thomson in 1890, were about to embark on a picnic. From the collection of CCHS

CHAPTER VI

PEOPLE AND PLACES

LEFT PAGE:

A distinguishing feature of the social life of early Carlton County was the extent to which ethnicity and church shaped activities. People were proud to be Americans, but they never forgot their cultural origins either. This photograph of Hannah Jarvi and Emma Viljanen, sisters and Thomson pioneers, celebrated their arrival from Sweden. From the collection of EHS

THE NATIVE PEOPLE, FIRST the Sioux and then the Ojibway, the explorers, first the French and then the English, the missionaries, the fur traders, the government agents, and the settlers—all step out of the pages of the social history of America. This diversity, like the economic and transportation history of the region, gives the county the rich character that it enjoys.

Little is known about the innkeepers along the Military Road, but their names alone tell us something. At Elkton, Bouillard, Gavioud, and Duquette, were obviously French-Canadian; at other inns were Jackson, Williams, Stull, and Dunsmore, who were probably English, possibly Yankees from New England; Dunphy was clearly Irish. Of this group the French-Canadians made an impact on the county that continues to the present. One postman of distinction was James Bungo, who was part Ojibway and part Black—the descendant of a slave owned by a British officer at the Sault. When logging operations entered the county a new

This Ojibway elder linked Carlton County of 1910 with the world of the St. Louis River valley before Europeans settled in the region. Octavie Morneau, photographer, from the collection of CCHS

Irish community was introduced, part of that great migration of Irish lumbermen from New Brunswick and Maine. Names like Mitchell, Sauntry, O'Brien, Cain, O'Meara, Scanlon, Dunlap, McNair, and Driscoll suggest their legacy.

One of the largest immigrant groups to establish a presence in the county were the Finns. The Finnish farmers who settled along the Midway River in 1873 created a distinctive culture that persists to this

Joseph Northrup and Angeline Peterson Northrup, of Sawyer, are shown with their daughter Julia and their dog Danger. Joseph Northrup attended the Carlisle Indian School in Pennsylvania around 1912 and was later active in church affairs and tribal politics on the Fond du Lac Reservation. From the collection of MHS

day. Northeastern Carlton County, particularly Esko and Cloquet, was strongly Finnish. By the twentieth century large numbers of Finnish farmers settled in the western region of the county, near Kettle River, Automba, Salo, and Cromwell. In 1905 Finns made up 75 percent of the population in Thomson, Kalevala, and eastern Lakeview townships and up to 50 percent in four others. In 1895 the Finnish born population in the county was between 6 and 8 percent, while by 1920 that proportion had grown to 11 percent.

A Swedish community settled in Carlton County, following the railroad north to the Moose Lake area, from the large Swedish settlements to the south. By the early twentieth century there were substantial

Swedish communities in five townships, making up between 25 percent and 50 percent of the inhabitants. Norwegians came to Carlton County in somewhat smaller numbers and were spread more evenly around the county. In 1905 both Norwegian-born and second generation reached their highest point, 907 and 1,577 respectively.

Germans first arrived along the rail line also, settling first near Barnum and Moose Lake. They became very successful farmers in the eastern and central parts of the county, particularly in the Wrenshall area and in Blackhoof township. Split Rock township saw a very large settlement of Polish farmers in the late nineteenth century. Cloquet and Scanlon also had a community of Poles, who by 1908 were able to establish St. Casimir's Catholic Church as a permanent place of worship.

Churches and schools were built very quickly after a community was established. In Carlton County both Roman Catholic and Lutheran Churches were founded in great number. Among the Lutherans, Swedish, Norwegian, and Finnish language groups tended to dominate, although there were several German Lutheran Churches as well. Only larger towns could support such other denominations as Presbyterian, Congregational, or Episcopal. As the twentieth century unfolded, a number of evangelical churches were founded also.

There were many country schools, although only the towns could offer high schools. These high schools became the center of many community activities, of which athletic teams and bands were only the most conspicuous. The larger towns quickly founded newspapers. Clubs, social groups, and fraternal organizations emerged in towns, providing the opportunity for the people to enjoy relaxation and beneficial activities.

Charles Ziebler and children. Charles and Augusta Ziebler had homesteaded along the Military Road in 1879 with the first group of German settlers, and in 1891 they moved into Barnum and opened the Ziebler Hotel. From the collection of CCHS

Isaac Walli, a Finnish immigrant, settled south of Wright in Lakeview Township and homesteaded. Walli broke his leg while trying to save Emil Rengo's sawmill in Automba and died in the great 1918 fire.
Courtesy of Ernest Walli

Our Lady of the Sacred Heart Church in Cloquet was the house of worship of many nationalities, but it was called the "French Catholic" Church, and indeed it held services in French for many years. This 1910 photograph of Arthenise Holmes shows the daughter of a prominent French speaking family, that of Rubin and Philamene Holmes, posed in her confirmation dress. Courtesy of Emily Soboleski

Cloquet also had a "Polish Catholic" Church, St. Casimir's. This photograph on the steps of the church shows a 1922 confirmation class, together with the bishop, priest, nuns, altar boys, and sponsors.
From the collection of CCHS

Pastor N. G. Nelson stands at the far left in the back row with the 1904 confirmation class from the Norwegian Lutheran Church of Moose Lake. From the collection of MLAHS

A less happy occasion is that of a funeral at the Norwegian Lutheran Church in Moose Lake in 1908. From the collection of MLAHS

Swedish Lutherans in Cloquet built the Zion Lutheran Church, shown here about 1910. This church was extensively remodeled and was to be re-dedicated on Sunday, October 13, 1918, but it was destroyed on October 12 by the great 1918 fire. Octavie Morneau, photographer, from the collection of CCHS

This charming summer wedding dinner celebrates the the Finnish-Swedish marriage of Saima Vasanoja and Segrid Syverson of Cromwell. From the collection of CCHS

Women from the Cloquet Coop and Women's Guild pose in flour-sack dresses worn for a play given at the Finn Hall. The working-class costumes and the hammer and sickle emblems indicate that radical social-political views, and an optimism about the Soviet Union, were not entirely absent from Carlton County in 1925, while the pearl necklaces worn by the young women suggest that class warfare was not taken too seriously either. McComb, photographer, from the collection of CCHS

These boys from the Moose Lake 4-H Club entered the Boys' Breadbaking at the Minnesota State Fair in 1920, and Royal Walters, second from the left, won First Prize. From the collection of MLAHS

The Boy Scouts provided fellowship, outdoor skills, and lots of fun. Here is Troop 1, Cloquet, the "White Pine" troop. H. F. Gillaspy-C. T. Cleveland, photographers, from the collection of CCHS

Carlton women had an opportunity to get together and to give public service through the Rebecca Lodge. From the collection of CCHS

The Moose Lake School Board in 1925, with H. M. Davis, Superintendent, David Anderson, C. F. Mahnke (with dunce cap), Albert Jacobson, David Almquist, and in front, Dr. F. R. Walters. From the collection of MLAHS

The family was the social structure around which much of the life of the county centered. The Ilstrup family of Cromwell is shown here in 1919—Audrey, Cora, and Lief—in an idyllic pose.

From the collection of CCHS

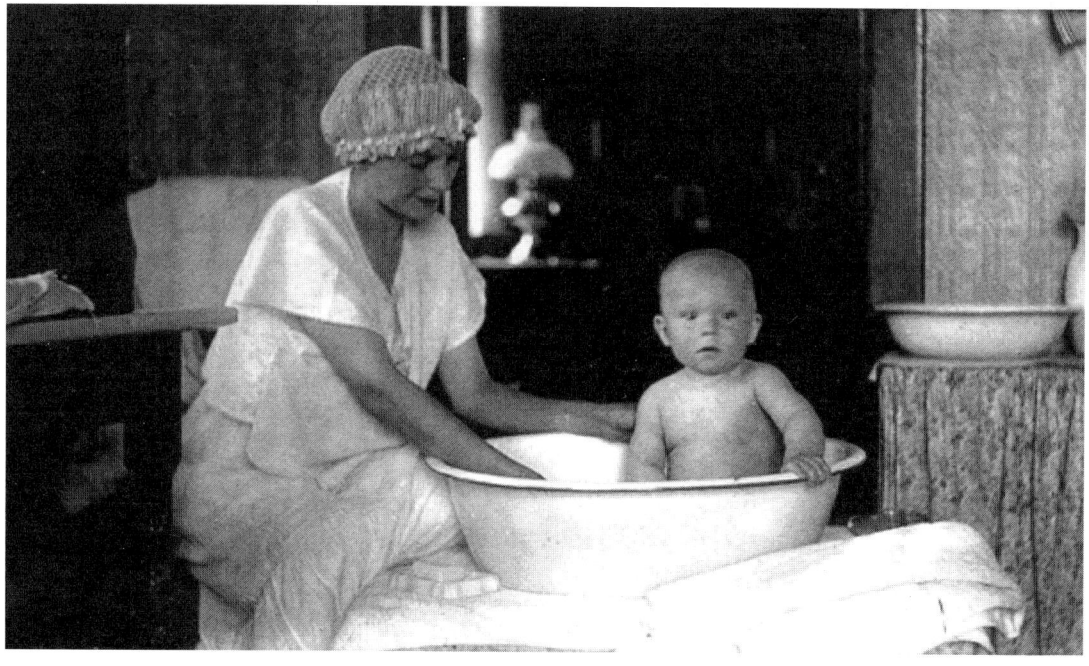

Babies! Here Gertrude Borglund of Wright gives her son Robert a bath in 1915. Harry Bergstrom, photographer, courtesy of Curt Borglund

Is this the old west? Actually, Charlotte Louise Newman and her cousin Helen Louise Solem are riding this burro in Cloquet in 1913 and posing for an itinerant photographer. Courtesy of Patricia Hampton

Women's rights were sought in various forms in the early twentieth century. Mary Winter did men's labor and she wore lumberjack's trousers as she did so. She was called Housa Maija, "Pants Mary," in Finnish and English, as Walter O'Meara remembered. From the collection of EHS

Ida Buxton from Thomson worked in Duluth as a streetcar operator during the First World War, and she also wore men's pants, as seen in this photograph on the far right. From the collection of CCHS

Is this a snowmobile? In the 1920s Nora Nilsen, the superintendent of rural schools, successfully visited her charges in this vehicle during the winters. From the collection of MLAHS

Less mechanical, but perhaps just as reliable for short trips in the winter, was this dog sled, used by Mrs. Fred Habhegger of Wrenshall. The dog pulled her at least five miles into town. From the collection of CCHS

A key figure in recording much of the life of the county was the professional photographer, Octavie Morneau. Born in Canada, she established a successful studio in Cloquet from 1902 to 1916. Octavie Morneau, photographer, from the collection of CCHS

CHAPTER VII

THE GREAT 1918 FIRES

LEFT PAGE:

Fire victim from the Moose Lake area being assisted by a nurse and a guardsman. William Bull, photographer, from the collection of CCHS

THE GREAT 1918 FIRES WERE a trauma for Carlton County. Within the entire region, 453 killed, 2,100 burned or injured, 11,328 displaced, 52,371 evacuated, 10 communities entirely destroyed and 17 damaged. One thousand five hundred square miles were burned, resulting in property damage estimated at $30,000,000, including some 4,089 houses, 6,366 barns, and innumerable farm animals. Cloquet, Moose Lake, the Fond du Lac Indian Reservation, Kettle River, and Automba, were destroyed, and many farms were consumed. The courts determined that the several fires had been started by the railroads. It is now known that unusual atmospheric conditions, most importantly a dramatic drop in humidity, may cause smoldering fires to explode. On October 12, 1918 these conditions occurred with cataclysmic results.

The fire that burned Cloquet started west of Brookston along the Great Northern Railroad tracks at a siding called Milepost 62. A passen-

The Cloquet train depot became a center for planning the evacuation of the town prior to the fire on Saturday, October 12, 1918. Depot Agent Lawrence Fauley was one of those who made sure that four trains were available to take between seven and eight thousand people to safety. The actual fatalities in Cloquet were fewer than six because so many people were taken out on the trains. From the collection of CCHS

ger train had started the fire on Thursday. On Saturday the fire flared up and burned east and south to Brookston and the Fond du Lac Indian Reservation. At about eight o'clock in the evening the fires burned through the Indian Village west of Cloquet and entered the yards of the Northern Lumber Company. Four relief trains had been organized in Cloquet, and took over 7,000 people to Duluth and Superior. Many were able to drive or walk to Carlton. A small number of people actually stayed in the town, some in the lake at Pinehurst Park, others on Dunlap Island or the north bank of the St. Louis River. Rudolph M. Weyerhaeuser and a handful of others fought the fire at the mills. The Northern was completely burned, the Cloquet Lumber Company sawmills were saved, but its facilities were destroyed, while the Johnson-Wentworth Lumber Company, the Northwest Paper Company, several other businesses, the Garfield School, and a few houses were spared. The rest of Cloquet was completely destroyed.

Fires had been smoldering along the Soo Line tracks west of Moose Lake since August. The railroad crews had not been able to extinguish these fires. On October 12th, the fires burned into some of the sawmills at Automba about four o'clock, causing the town to explode in flames. The fire continued southeast into the farming settlement in Split Rock township and forced people to seek shelter in the Split Rock River or to flee farther south. Efforts to fight the fire west of Kettle River were defeated when the fire broke through the fire lines, and by six o'clock in the evening it was moving rapidly southeast toward the town. A relief train from Moose Lake rescued a number of people, others took refuge in the Kettle River below the railroad bridge. However, of those who attempted to drive south to Moose Lake along Highway 73, many were overtaken by the flames at "Dead Man's Curve," where the road turned sharply east. Moose Lake was doomed also. Several hundred people found protection in Moosehead Lake. The mayor of Moose Lake, Richard T. Hart, who spent the night under the bridge in Kettle River, walked to Sturgeon Lake to wire the Governor for help.

Could the county recover? After numerous meetings the Cloquet sawmill owners decided to pool the resources of the three big companies and carry on in somewhat reduced circumstances. The paper mill and the match and box factories reopened quickly. The city was rebuilt, much of it within a year's time, but the new city was smaller. Although suffering terribly the rural communities revived as well. Moose Lake and Kettle River were rebuilt. Helped by the Relief Commission,

This photograph of the old City Hall and Jail shows the extent of the destruction in most of Cloquet. This photograph was taken on Tuesday, October 15, three days after the fire. People had started to come back and the flag was flying, but the situation still looked very grim. From the collection of the St. John's Abbey Archives

The fire destroyed the structure here, but left the picket fence behind it. Hugh McKenzie, photographer, from the collection of CCHS

people came back to their farms. The county survived, but the Great 1918 Fires left a mark on both those who lived through them and on subsequent generations.

The Duluth Armory was made into a refugee center by Saturday evening, October 12th. When it had reached its capacity, other buildings in Duluth were made available for refugees to sleep and eat. The Armory remained the center for locating and assisting people for days afterwards. From the collection of MLAHS

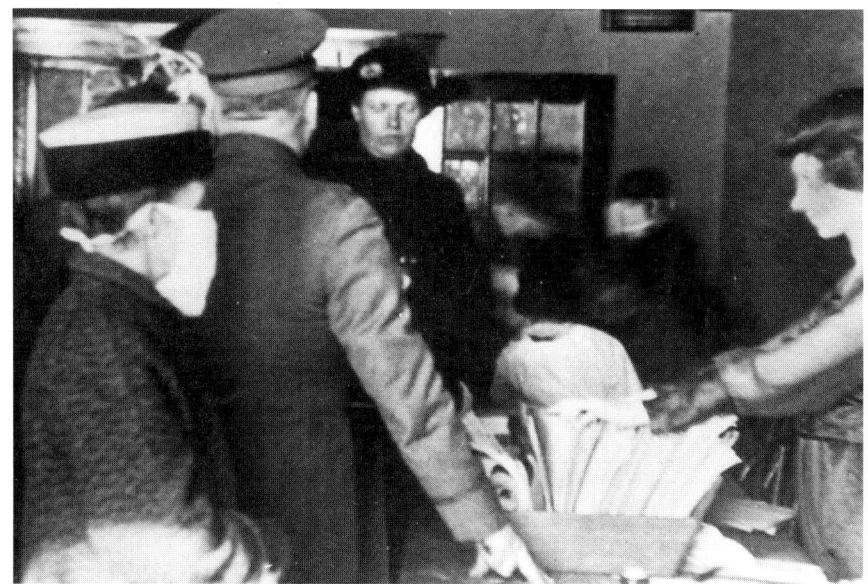

Driven by northwest winds, the fire that burned Cloquet had previously swept through the Fond du Lac Indian Reservation. The survivors were forced to live in tents and shelters upon their return. From the collection of CCHS

Relief shelters, generally called "Red Cross shacks," were built throughout the fire area. Farm people were also given lumber to build barns and other farm buildings in order to start farming as soon as possible. Here the workers take a break while putting up a "Red Cross shack." Hugh McKenzie, photographer, from the collection of CCHS

Within a matter of days after the fire, the Minnesota Forest Fires Relief Commission was created. Food, supplies, and the lumber to build a small shanty were provided to all those who lost their homes. This photograph of the ruined Presbyterian and Catholic Churches shows the general devastation and, in the foreground, the new relief shelters being built. From the collection of CCHS

Moose Lake, like Cloquet, was destroyed by the fire. From the collection of MLAHS

PICTURED BELOW:
Most of the people in Moose Lake found safety in Moosehead Lake. Not only did people drive their cars into the lake, but one person was brought directly from the operating room to the lake and survived both ordeals. Hugh McKenzie, photographer, from the collection of CCHS

Over half of the 453 people killed were in the Moose Lake, Kettle River, Automba, Split Rock area. The fire caught these people quite unprepared, and their rural isolation made escape difficult. Many attempted to save themselves by seeking shelter in root cellars or wells. This was often disastrous because the oxygen was consumed by the fire, causing the people to suffocate. Eight of the nine children of Nick and Hulda Koivisto, along with eight others, died in a neighbor's root cellar as the parents and the neighbor stayed outside, and survived, while attempting to protect the root cellar. Hugh McKenzie, photographer, from the collection of CCHS

At least twenty died at "Dead Man's Curve," fifty-nine at Eckman's corner, fifteen to twenty volunteer fire fighters west of Kettle River, sixteen in the Koivisto-Niemi root cellar, fourteen in the Soderberg root cellar, seven in the Williams root cellar, and numerous others in different circumstances in the region. The Minnesota Home Guard from the southern part of the state did much of the work of finding the bodies, putting them in coffins, and making arrangements for their burial in Moose Lake. Here they are seen unloading coffins. William Bull, photographer, from the collection of MLAHS

The task of retrieving and making provisions for the dead was a grizzly one. Hugh McKenzie, photographer, from the collection of CCHS

A mass grave was prepared just east of Moose Lake for many of the fire victims. Governor J. A. A. Burnquist came from St. Paul to attend the funerals, inspect the fire damage, and get the relief commission started. From the collection of MLAHS

With the help of the Minnesota Forest Fires Relief Commission, Moose Lake area fire sufferers did return and start farming again. From the collection of MLAHS

A box car, taken off its wheels, was made to serve as the Northern Pacific depot in Moose Lake. Fred Levie, photographer, from the collection of MLAHS

Large numbers of the Minnesota Home Guard served in the Moose Lake area, and their assistance was needed until early 1919. From the collection of MLAHS

This famous photograph of Cloquet was taken about five years after the fire and gives no suggestion that all of the houses and buildings were entirely new. From the collection of CCHS

PICTURED BELOW:

Map of the fire area which also showed the locations of the key cases in the litigation against the railroads and the government. From a booklet, "Minnesota Forest Fires, 1918," Franklin D. Roosevelt Library, Hyde Park, New York

Many of the fire sufferers attempted to sue the railroads and the U.S. Railroad Administration for damages that were held to have been caused by fires traced to the railroads. The railroad companies sent their own lawyers into the fire areas to take statements from witnesses. This photograph shows the railroad lawyers visiting the Kettle River area and the Soo Line train in which they stayed. From the collection of CCHS

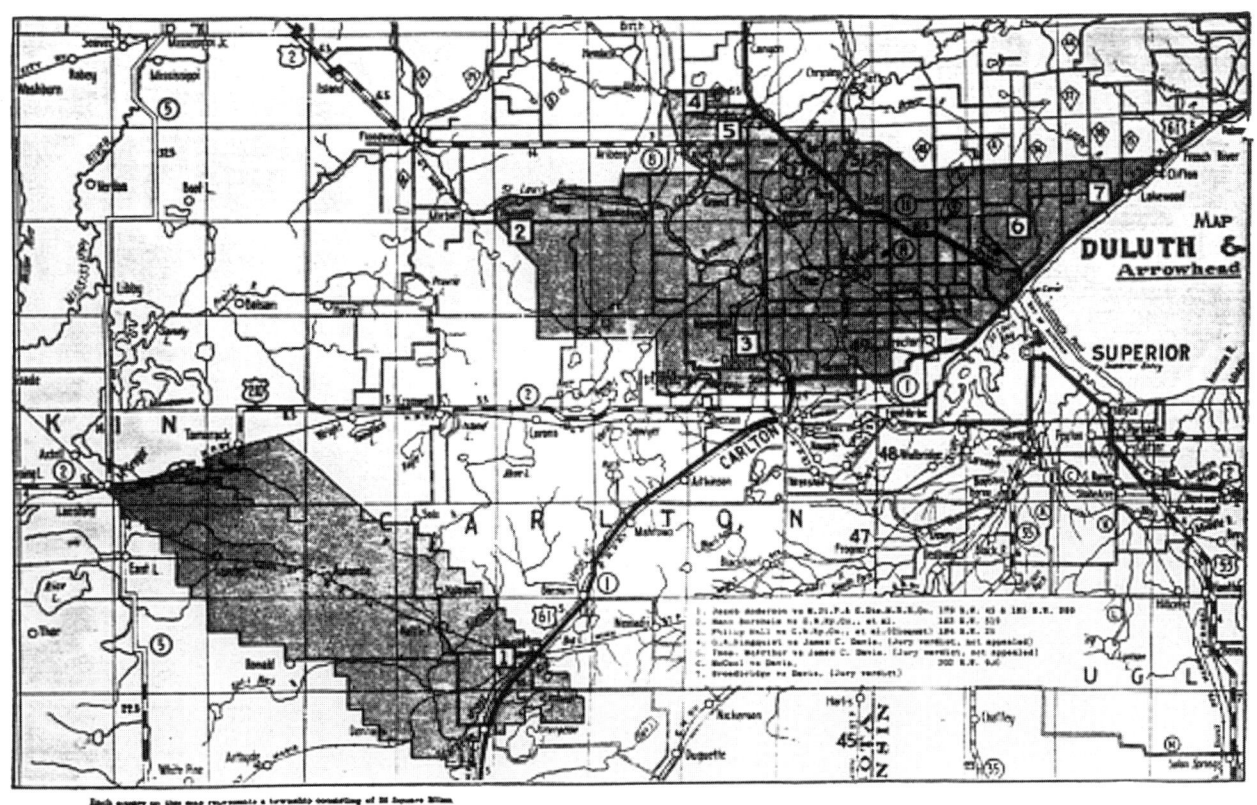

CHAPTER VIII

RECREATION

LEFT PAGE:

Did you think riding bicycles on country trails was an idea of the 1980s? Here Anna Olson and Lucille McCabe of Moose Lake go on a day's outing in 1901. From the collection of MLAHS

A CENTRAL FEATURE OF life in America has been the county fair, and Carlton County was no exception. The first Carlton County Fair was held in Barnum in 1891, and the Esko Community Fair was started in 1929. The original purpose of the fair was to promote agriculture through awards for the best livestock and crops, although this naturally expanded to include prizes for such activities as handicrafts, stitchery, and cooking. These competitions attracted a large number of women and men. Horse racing, athletic contests, and feats of strength and skill were also a major part of the fair, as were the entertaining grand stand shows.

The Fourth of July celebrations were a summer high point for townsfolk. The festivities always started with a parade that featured bands, as well as the mayor, town council, veterans from the Civil War or the First World War, and many local organizations. The parade would be followed by speeches honoring the occasion, carnival rides, a band concert, and games. Although there were generally foot races for children, the big event would be a baseball game staring either the city team or the high school team. In keeping with its logging origins, in Cloquet log rolling, or birling, competitions would be held in Pinehurst Park. The town proudly claimed several men's and women's world champion log rollers. Fireworks, then as now, would end the day's celebrations.

The Carlton County Fair in Barnum was one of the high points of every summer, and race day was a main attraction. The harness racing event is about to begin. The crowd has formed along the fence, and you can almost hear the bugler sound "First Call." From the collection of CCHS

Although record players and radios were increasingly available in the 1920s and 1930s, people still expected to make their own music. Every family with any pretensions attempted to provide piano lessons for their children. The larger high schools offered instruction in band instruments, and enormous local pride was generated by the quality of the high school band. The opportunity to sing was even more available in church choirs, school glee clubs, and private singing groups, such as the Viking Chorus in Cloquet. Dance bands also provided music locally, and Carlton County had a remarkable number of them. The 1920s and 1930s enjoyed something of a dance craze, with formal balls, high school dances, wedding dances, club hops, country dances in town halls, and many other occasions. No doubt part of this was inspired by the celebrated "Jazz Age," but part of it also grew out of the eastern

The Carlton County Sportsman's Club's booth at the fair was typical of many displays. Olson Studio, from the collection of CCHS

106 ✤ Reflections Of Our Past

European traditions of the Finnish and Polish communities of the county, with their famous polka music.

Sports, somewhat like music, recruited many of its participants from the schools. Every high school in the county had some kind of sports program. The basic sport was baseball, which of course was played both in and out of school. The larger schools could offer football and, those with gymnasiums, boy's and girl's basketball. Sports for adults also thrived. Baseball was the most popular, and every town had a baseball team to play on Saturday or Sunday afternoon, but many also played tennis and golf.

Hunting, fishing, and boating were enormously popular activities in Carlton County. Deer hunting was particularly good in the western part of the county and south of Wrenshall. Partridge and ducks could be shot in the autumn as well. Stream fishing was always good, and lake fishing abounded. On the larger lakes fishing boats could be rented. Chub Lake, Big Lake, and Moosehead Lake had elaborate bathhouse facilities, so that it was possible to have family outings and church picnics for large crowds of people, but many other lakes became popular also.

One of the greatest recreational resources in Carlton County has been Jay Cooke State Park. This park grew out of the gift of the heirs of the Northern Pacific financier Jay Cooke. In 1915 some 2,350 acres of land along the St. Louis River valley were given to the State of Minnesota. A road was begun along the old railroad grade in 1916. Favorite attractions at Jay Cooke Park were the picnic areas and the suspension bridge across the dalles of the St. Louis River. This bridge was washed out from time to time by the spring flood waters, but it was regularly rebuilt and provided a spectacular view of the river, as well as access to the south bank and the trails on that side. In the the 1930s and 1940s more land was acquired, eventually expanding the park to over 11,000 acres. The historical associations of the St. Louis River with Indians, explorers, and fur traders; the natural beauty of the region, with its geologic formation, its thick forest cover, and its abundant wildlife; the diverse recreational facilities for picnics, games, and hikes—all combined to make Jay Cooke State Park a treasure for Carlton County.

On Memorial Day in Cloquet 1915, the fiftieth anniversary of the end of the Civil War, these county veterans of the Grand Army of the Republic were the center of attraction. Sitting in the car are McKean Smith, A. S. Clemons, Frank Lenier, and Mr. Bowman. From the collection of CCHS

Imaginative floats delighted the spectators at Fourth of July parades. In 1926 the Cloquet Public Library float won the prize. From the collection of CCHS

The Cloquet City Band, under the direction of L. D. Gerin during the 1920s and 1930s, performed brilliantly both in parades and in concerts at the band shell in Pinehurst Park. From the collection of CCHS

108 ❧ Reflections Of Our Past

The Fourth of July celebrations in Cloquet were unique because of the log rolling or "birling" contests that were held in the pond at Pinehurst Park. These very log rolling skills were used driving logs down the rivers to the mills. This large 1910 crowd shows how popular these log rolling events were. In the water is a bateau to assist the contestants get on the logs. From the collection of CCHS

The log rollers, wearing calked boots, would spin the log in the water at top speed (as shown here) and attempt to throw their opponent off by stopping the log dead in the water or reversing the spin. Cloquet had many champion birlers, including Will Delyea, Joe Connor, Lawrence Bergeron, and Laura Marchand Hebert. Olson Studio, from the collection of CCHS

In Carlton County you did not need a public holiday to have a parade. Here Mogan McClay is pushing Finley Palmer from Carlton to Cloquet in a wheelbarrow to pay off a political debt. Alfred E. Smith, and McClay, had lost in the presidential election of 1928. W. H. Hassing, photographer, from the collection of CCHS

Carlton County, Minnesota ❋ 109

This 1903 photograph of the Cloquet High School girls' basketball team demonstrates that women's athletics had an important place from early on. Octavie Morneau, photographer, from the collection of CCHS

The crowd watched intently as Moose Lake played Wrenshall in this 1912 game at the county fair. From the collection of CCHS

The Cromwell baseball team was ready to play ball in 1913. From the collection of CCHS

The Carlton Bulldogs of 1930 included Cliff Haubner and George Gillespie (fourth and fifth from the left, back row) and Bob McFarland (seventh from the left). From the collection of CCHS

Horseshoe pitching was always fun at a picnic or the fair. In 1930 Harry Hard won the Silver Horseshoe in Carlton County. Olson Studio, from the collection of CCHS

These gracious young ladies, Annie Mae Woodworth, Marie Watkins, Margaret Oldenberg, Winona Watkins, and Maytie Beattie, are ready for a game of tennis. From the collection of CCHS

Ida Morse of Cromwell, with fur coat and muffler, is ready to brave the elements on Island Lake with skates in 1912. From the collection of CCHS

Organized hockey did not get started in Cloquet until 1935, but the Barnum boys could always get together with sticks and a puck and start a game of shinny. From the collection of CCHS

Here the Cloquet Saturday Musical and Choral Society perform "The 13th Chair" in 1925. From the collection of CCHS

The workers of the Berst-Forster-Dixfield Match Factory produced "Beauty and the Beast." Olson Studio, from the collection of CCHS

Carlton County, Minnesota ❧ 113

The Viking Chorus was a distinctive part of cultural life in Cloquet. It remained active right through the 1950s. From the collection of CCHS

Dancing became very popular in the 1920s, with the result that dance bands flourished. Skelly's Orchestra was a popular Moose Lake band.

From the collection of MLAHS

The many lakes and streams in the county provided excellent fishing. However, we may never again see sturgeon such as these (weighing from 35 to 57 pounds), caught in Moosehead Lake. From the collection of MLAHS

These deer hunters have good reason to be pleased with their efforts. Although many areas in the county offered good hunting, these deer were shot south of Wrenshall in 1910. From the collection of CCHS

Boating and cottages have been a source of recreation in Carlton County from about the turn of the century. Here three teachers from Wright are rowing at Tamarack Lake in the LADY RIPPLES, a traditional, clinker-built praam made by Fred B. Bergstrom. Harry Bergstrom, photographer, from the collection of Curt Borglund

This large group was enjoying a day at Chub Lake in about 1914. From the collection of CCHS

Jay Cooke State Park has been a favorite recreational area since it was created in 1915. One of the most attractive features of the park is the swinging bridge across the river, shown here in 1925. From the collection of CCHS

CHAPTER IX

LIFE IN CARLTON COUNTY

LEFT PAGE:

The telephone switchboard in Cloquet was run by the "operator" who rang the number for you. From the collection of CCHS

ONE OF THE REMARKABLE facets of life in Carlton County in the 1920s and 1930s was the continued growth of the agricultural community. The destruction of many farm animals in the fires may have presented an opportunity to rebuild the dairy herds with purebred cattle. Loren J. Beck, Jessie Doan, and Carl Duesler, of the Barnum area, as well as H. C. Hanson, were largely responsible for encouraging the adoption of high quality Guernsey cows. County Agents, University of Minnesota Extension Service, 4-H Clubs, breeders associations, and others were all helpful. By 1935 it could be said that 80 percent of all the dairy herds in the county were purebred Guernsey or Holstein cows. The result was that dairy products from all over the county, became famous throughout the state. Poultry and egg production paralleled that of dairy farming in bringing genuine prosperity to Carlton County farmers in the 1920s. Contrary to the national trends, rural population grew in Carlton County. Undiminished by the

The First World War brought many Carlton County young men into uniform and took them "over there." Harry Bergstrom, photographer, courtesy of Curt Borglund

1918 fires, the number of people in agriculture grew from 1,938 in 1920 to 2,889 in 1930—a substantial increase.

Part of the success of economic life in both rural and urban areas in the 1920s can be attributed to the growth of Cooperative Societies. Cooperatives had their first appearance in the county as produce marketing devices for farmers, but in the 1920s and 1930s cooperatives were also organized to provide retail stores and a variety of other services. Kettle River started a telephone cooperative in 1908 and an electrical power company through the Rural Electrification Administration in 1935. By the 1930s the Cloquet Cooperative Society was the largest in the United States.

The industrial economy in the county grew in the 1920s also, although it began to take a different form. The lumber industry would never again be what it had once been. Sawmill operations were halted in the 1930s and were gradually succeeded by the wood fiber industries. The Northwest Paper Company expanded and upgraded, adding new paper machines and pulp facilities. In 1924 it stopped making newsprint and concentrated on manufacturing high quality papers. The Weyerhaeuser directors set in motion the building of the Wood Conversion Company

Anna Dickie Olesen, the wife of Peter Olesen, superintendent of the Cloquet Public Schools, became a force in the Minnesota Democratic Party. A brilliant public speaker in the Chautauqua circuit, she received the nomination of the Democratic Party to run for the U.S. Senate in 1922 against the Republican incumbent, Frank B. Kellogg. The Farmer-Labor candidate, Henrik Shipstead, won, but Mrs. Olesen ran a strong campaign and was the first woman in America to run for the Senate as the candidate of a major party. Courtesy of the Gerin family

on the site of the old Northern Lumber Company, to manufacture wood fiber insulation and other building products with new technology. The box factory closed, but the match mill was purchased by the Diamond Match Company and by 1929 new buildings and machinery were built. The construction boom that followed the 1918 fires brought prosperity

In the summer of 1927 President Calvin Coolidge spent his summer holidays south of Superior, Wisconsin, near the Brule River. Members of the Carlton County 4-H Clubs, together with a prize winning calf, were taken to meet him. Courtesy of Juella Iverson

to many skilled tradesmen, contractors, and the brick making plants in Wrenshall. However, the Great Depression cut deeply into all new building in the region.

Carlton County with its mixed economy did not suffer as much during the Great Depression as some parts of the country (in 1933 some 25 percent of the national work force was unemployed). When Franklin D. Roosevelt became president in 1933 a number of programs were started for the purpose of easing the effects of the depression. One of the earliest of these "New Deal" agencies was the Civilian Conservation Corps. It was designed to get unemployed young men off the streets, teach them some skills, and employ them on conservation projects. In 1933 camps were set up at Jay Cooke State Park and Big Lake. These young men planted trees, fought forest fires, and made major improvements to the trails and buildings at Jay Cooke State Park. Several other major New

H. C. Hanson, the owner of the Barnum Creamery, whose sleek delivery truck is seen here, improved the sales and profits for county farmers by encouraging better breeds of cattle and chickens. From the collection of CCHS

Deal projects were started in the county, such as the construction of the Highway 33 bridge over the St. Louis River in Cloquet by the Works Progress Administration. Moose Lake was selected as the site for a new State Hospital, which made an important contribution to the life of the town.

By the decade of the 1930s, despite the dislocation of the 1918 Fires and the Great Depression, Carlton County was shaped as it would remain for the next fifty years. New forest industries became a central part of the economy of Cloquet and the county. The railroads also had left their stamp on the county. Every town had been built along some railroad line. The look of those towns, especially those which had been rebuilt after the 1918 fires, was also fixed for the next several generations—comfortable towns with brick stores and schools and wood frame houses, with gracious churches, wide streets, and green parks. Farm life, tied in many ways to the railroads, also reached its peak by the early 1930s. The people embodied a chapter in American social history. Ojibway on the Fond du Lac Indian Reservation, Finns among the earliest farmers, Irish and French-Canadian following the lumber trade, Swedes and Norwegians

moving north along the railroads from southern Minnesota, Germans, Belgians, and Poles settling in the south central farmlands—all of this had been threatened first by the Great 1918 Fires and then by the Great Depression, but the roots of Carlton County went too deep.

PICTURED ABOVE:

Competition at the Carlton County Fair for the best calves was one way to encourage careful breeding. Here the Mahtowa Calf Club exhibits at the fair in Barnum. From the collection of CCHS

LEFT PAGE:

Cooperatives organized both marketing facilities and retail stores. This photograph shows a large meeting of the Kettle River Coop Creamery Association in 1929. Cliff Studio photograph, from the collection of CCHS

The Carlton County Farm Bureau, with its local branches like this one at Twin Lakes, provided another means to encourage innovative farm practices. From the collection of CCHS

A farm auction, like this one in the Moose Lake area in the early 1920s, was the way to sell the elaborate equipment accumulated on a farm, and the best way for a purchaser to get a good deal. From the collection of MLAHS

Every decade or so there is a winter to remember. February 22nd and 23rd of 1924 saw an incredible snowfall. Here Cloquet digs out. From the collection of CCHS

In the aftermath of the 1918 forest fires, Ranger stations were built in both Moose Lake and Cloquet. This 1931 photograph shows the forest rangers still in the uniform of riding britches, lace-top boots, and campaign hats. From the collection of MHS

Uniforms were common symbols of employment. These smartly dressed men were the Cloquet postmen. They are, standing, Clarence Scheibe (later postmaster), William Boyer, Edwin C. Nelson, Joseph Pastika, and Harry Nordquist, and kneeling, Harry Kaner, mayor of Cloquet in the 1930s. From the collection of CCHS

PICTURED BELOW:
One of the major events in the county was the opening of the Moose Lake State Hospital in 1937. P. M. Mehl, photographer, from the collection of CCHS

This 1907 Baldwin locomotive was one of the workhorses of the Duluth and Northeastern Railroad. Here General Superintendent Charles A. Jensen gives the engine crew their orders before heading out from the yards on Dunlap Island. From the collection of MHS

The Rotary Club of Cloquet provided generous leadership for the community. Among its many service activities, the Rotary Club struck a committee which eventually led to the founding of the Carlton County Historical Society. Olson Studio photograph, from the collection of CCHS

The Cloquet Cooperative Society became the largest in the United States. The Coop had two grocery and hardware stores in Cloquet, and also stores in Esko and Mahtowa, not to mention a lumber and feed store, a petroleum distributorship, a funeral home, and a credit union. This huge store was Coop No. 1, where you could buy anything from dried fish to horse harnesses and be served in either English or Finnish.

From the collection of CCHS

Finnish culture was celebrated in a number of ways in Carlton County and music was one of them. One of the most popular Finnish musicians was Viola Turpeinen, shown here, second from the left, helping to put up hay at a Cloquet area farm. Her husband, William Syrjala, a musician in his own right, grew up in Cloquet. From the collection of CCHS

One of several large skilled trades unions in Cloquet was the United Brotherhood of Carpenters and Jointers. From the collection of CCHS

Protest and discontent over economic conditions did flare up in the 1930s. Here a group of farmers staged a demonstration in the Carlton County Court House, inventing the "sit-in" twenty years before the civil rights movement coined the phrase. From the collection of MHS

One of the agencies that the federal government created to deal with the Great Depression was the Civilian Conservation Corps. Carlton County had two C.C.C. camps, one at Jay Cooke State Park and the other at Big Lake. This is a detail of a 1934 photograph of the Big Lake Camp. G. O. Mehl, photographer, from the collection of CCHS

It can be argued that as the decade of the 1930s closed, a new era was about to begin. A harbinger of that change was powered flight, both civil and military. At that pivotal moment, it is comforting to think of Roscoe O. Raiter, more generally remembered as a prominent Cloquet pharmacist and businessman, flying the mail in a biplane from the old grass covered Cloquet Airport to Wold-Chamberlain Field (now the Minneapolis-St. Paul International Airport) as part of National Air Mail Week in 1938. From the collection of CCHS

PICTURED BELOW:

Scanlon. If America, and Carlton County, were poised on the edge of great change, it is pleasant to look back on life in Carlton County and find the homely virtues of the middle west embodied in its photographic history. Nelson Freeman, photographer, from the collection of CCHS

Carlton County, Minnesota ✿ 137

FURTHER READING

Anderson, David E. MOOSE LAKE AREA HISTORY. N.p., 1965.

_____. MOOSE LAKE AREA HISTORY: VOLUME II, 1918 TO THE PRESENT. Moose Lake, 1989.

Beck, Bennet A. BRIEF HISTORY OF THE PIONEERS OF THE CROMWELL MINNESOTA AREA. N.p., 1967.

CARLTON COUNTY CENTENNIAL, 1857–1957. N.p., 1962.

Carroll, Francis M. CROSSROADS IN TIME: A HISTORY OF CARLTON COUNTY, MINNESOTA. Cloquet, 1987.

_____. READING AND RESEARCH: A SUPPLEMENT TO CROSSROADS IN TIME: A HISTORY OF CARLTON COUNTY, MINNESOTA. Cloquet, 1989.

Carroll, Francis M., and Franklin R. Raiter. THE FIRES OF AUTUMN: THE CLOQUET-MOOSE LAKE DISASTER OF 1918. St. Paul, 1990.

Federal Writers' Project. THE W.P.A. GUIDE TO THE MINNESOTA ARROWHEAD COUNTRY. New introduction by Francis M. Carroll. St. Paul, 1988 [first published 1941].

Harrison, Frederick G. CINDERS AND TIMBER. N.p., 1967.

Hemingson, Ray E. DEATH BY FIRE: THE STORY OF THE GREAT NORTHEASTERN MINNESOTA FOREST FIRE. Waupaca, 1985.

Manni, E. E. KETTLE RIVER, AUTOMBA, KALEVALA AND SURROUNDING AREA HISTORY. Tamarack, 1978.

Niemi, Harriette. "Awfullest Fire Horror in State's History." Cloquet, n.d.

Olsen, Harold S. FROM WHITE PINE TO CLOVER. Tamarack, 1983.

O'Meara, Walter. THE TREES WENT FORTH. New York, 1947.

_____. WE MADE IT THROUGH THE WINTER: MEMOIRS OF MINNESOTA BOYHOOD. St. Paul, 1974.

Sommer, Barbara. "THE CITY THAT REALLY CAME BACK:" CLOQUET AND THE FIRES OF 1918. Cloquet, 1985.

Swanson, S. Hjalmar. A HISTORY OF MAHTOWA. N.p., n.d.

INDEX

A
Addington, Ray, 64
Almquist, David, 87
Anderson, David, 87
Andreas Miller Lumber Company, 55
Apostolic Lutheran Church of Esko, 42
Armstrong, Ed., 44
Atkinson, 32
Automba, 52, 67, 80, 82, 93, 99

B
Balton, Lorraine, 64
Barker, 53
Barnum, 22, 32, 33, 40, 46, 47, 52, 53, 59, 63, 64, 66, 75, 81, 105, 106, 112, 125
Barnum Creamery, 47, 123
BARNUM GAZETTE, 8
Barnum, George G., 22, 64
Baumann, Julius B., 69
Beattie, Maytie, 112
Beck, Loren J., 119
Berg, Chris, 57
Bergeron, Lawrence, 109
Bergstrom, Fred B., 116
Berst-Forster-Dixfield Match Factory, 60, 113
Bethel Swedish Lutheran Church, 32
Big Lake, 107, 122, 136
Blackhoof, 28, 45, 48, 57, 67, 81
Borglund, Gertrude, 88
Borglund, Robert, 88
Bowman, Mr., 108
Boy Scouts, 86
Boyer, William, 68, 129
Brooks-Scanlon Lumber Company, 31, 53, 67
Brophy, Mr., 64
Bungo, James, 79
Burnquist, J. A. A., Governor, 101
Buxton, Ida, 90

C
Cameron, Dan, 23
Cameron, Emily Dunn, 23
Cameron, Grace, 23
Carlson, Ida, 69
Carlson, John G., 48
Carlton County Fair, 105, 106, 125
Carlton County Farm Bureau, 126
Carlton County Historical Society, 75, 131
Carlton County Sportsman's Club, 106
Carlton Feed and Livery, 44
Carlton Horse Market, 43
Carlton Motor Company, 71
Carlton School, 77
Carlton, 25, 28, 29, 30, 36, 41, 44, 53, 65, 67, 70, 75, 87, 94, 109, 111
Carlton, Reuben C., Colonel, 18, 19
Chub Lake, 107, 117
Civilian Conservation Corps, 136
Clark and Jackson Camp, 52
Clemons, A. S., 108
Clemons, Augustus, 40
Cloquet City Band, 108
Cloquet Cooperative Society, 85, 120, 132
Cloquet High School, 73, 110
Cloquet Lumber Company, 52, 53, 94
Cloquet Public Library, 75, 108
Cloquet Saturday Musical and Choral Society, 113
Cloquet, 24, 28, 30, 34, 35, 40, 41, 57, 58, 59, 60, 62, 67, 68, 71, 72, 74, 75, 80, 81, 82, 85, 86, 89, 91, 93, 94, 95, 96, 98, 103, 106, 108, 109, 112, 114, 118, 128, 129, 132, 133, 134-135 137
Clover Dale Colony, 49
Connor, Joe, 109
Cooke, Jay, 28, 54, 107
Cooke, Jay, State Park, 107, 117, 122, 136
Cooperative Societies, 85, 120, 132
Corona, 15
Coryell, Yella, 19
Cromwell, 15, 43, 52, 66, 80, 85, 88, 110, 112
Culver, J. B., Colonel, 29
Culver, Mr., 67

D

Davis, H. M., 87
Delyea, Will, 109
Diamond Match Company, 121
Duesler, Carl, 119
Duluth and Northeastern Railroad, 36, 53, 130
Duluth and Winnipeg Railroad, 31, 67
Dunlap Island, 36, 52, 94, 130

E

East End Hat and Art Shoppe, 72
Elkton, 27, 65, 79
Erickson, William, 45
Eschelman, J. H., 76
Esko Community Fair, 105
Esko, 40, 67, 80, 132
Esko, Alexander, 67

F

Fauley, Lawrence, 94
Felgen, Mike, 22
Fond du Lac, 16, 18, 39, 40, 62
Fond du Lac Indian Reservation, 16, 17, 18, 19, 52, 74, 80, 93, 94, 96, 123
Foster, Thomas, Dr., 29
4-H Club, 86, 119, 122
Franklin, Joe, 68

G

Garfield School, 94
Gerin, L. D., 108
Gillespie, George, 111
Goman, Charlie, 44
Goodell, Luella, 64
Gourneau, Joseph, 16
Grasshopper, Mrs., 17
Gray, Albert, 56
Great 1918 Fires, 41, 93, 96, 124
Great Northern Railroad, 30, 31, 35, 36, 67, 93
Gus Moser's Meat Market, 70

H

Habhegger, 63
Habhegger, Fred J., 53
Habhegger, Fred, Mrs., 91
Habhegger, John, 45
Hanson, Hans Carl, 40, 41, 46, 47, 119, 123
Hard, Harry, 111
Hart, Richard T., 95

Haubner, Cliff, 111
Hebert, Laura Marchand, 109
Hecker, Clara, 64
Holmes, Arthenise, 82
Holmes, Clara, 71
Holmes, Philamene, 82
Holmes, Rubin, 82
Holy Family Church, 18, 74
Holy Names of Jesus and Mary, 69
Holyoke, 67
Homar, Roman, Father, 18

I

Ilstrup, Audrey, 88
Ilstrup, Cora, 88
Ilstrup, Lief, 88
Indian Village, 18, 74, 94
Iverson, 66

J

Jacobson, Albert, 87
Jacobson, S. A., 70
Jarvi, Hannah, 79
Jensen, Charles A., 130
Johnson town, 68
Johnson, B., Miss, 73
Johnson, Hannah, 64
Johnson, Myrt, 72
Johnson, Samuel S., 53
Johnson-Wentworth Lumber Company, 53, 57, 94

K

Kalevala township, 80
Kaner, Harry, 129
Kettle River Coop Creamery Association, 47, 125
Kettle River, 32, 47, 52, 67, 80, 93, 94, 95, 99, 103
Knife Falls Lumber Company, 52
Knife Falls, 28, 52, 68
Knutilas's Store, 66
Koivisto, Hulda, 99
Koivisto, Nick, 99
Korhonen, Charles, 32, 47
Kreiger, Louise, 64
Kubat, Joseph, 43

L

Lake Superior and Mississippi Railroad, 16, 28, 40
Lakeview township, 80, 82
Lampinen, Emil, 47

LaVoi, George, 44
Lee, Mayme, 64
Leimer, Louis, 59
Lenier, Frank, 108
Lindmark, Irene, 66
Lindmark, John, 66
Livingston, Russell, 47
Lower. H. K., 67

M
Mahnke, C. F., 87
Mahtowa Calf Club, 125
Mahtowa, 40, 52, 66, 69, 132
Mallinen, Abraham, Reverend, 42
Marks, John, 19
Mattson, Andrew, 45
McCabe, Lucille, 105
McClay, Mogan, 109
McFarland, Bob, 111
Mesabe Southern Railway, 53
Michaelson, Lotti Olson, 69
Midway River, 19, 39, 40, 55
Military Road, 27, 28, 30, 79
Miller, Andreas M., 16, 51, 55
Minnesota and North Wisconsin Railroad, 31
Minnesota Forest Fires Relief Commission, 95, 97, 101
Minnesota Home Guard, 100, 102
Moose Lake Area Historical Society, 33
Moose Lake School Board, 87
Moose Lake State Hospital, 123, 130
Moose Lake Tile and Pottery Company, 63
Moose Lake, 12, 21, 33, 38, 42, 48, 52, 56, 63, 65, 66, 67, 70, 75, 80, 81, 83, 86, 92, 93, 94, 95, 98, 99, 100, 101, 102, 105, 110, 114, 123, 127, 128
Moosehead Lake, 95, 98, 107, 115
Morneau, Octavie, 91
Morrision, D. George, 16
Morse, Ida, 112
Mortensen Saloon, 72

N
Nelson town, 68
Nelson, C. N., and Company, 24, 53
Nelson, Charles N., 52
Nelson, Edwin C., 129
Nelson, N. G., Pastor, 83
Newman, Charlotte Louise, 89
Newman, Willie, 69

Nilsen, Nora, 90
Nordquist, Harry, 129
Northern Lumber Company, 24, 53, 57, 59, 94, 121
Northern Pacific Junction, 19, 20, 30, 51, 52, 65
Northern Pacific Railroad, 15, 16, 25, 26, 28, 29, 30, 31, 32, 34, 36, 52, 66, 68, 102, 107
Northrup, Angeline Peterson, 80
Northrup, Joseph, 80
Northrup, Julia, 80
Northwest Paper Company, 53, 59, 60, 94, 120
Norwegian Lutheran Church of Moose Lake, 83

O
O'Meara, Walter, 58, 89
Ojibway, 16, 17, 39, 40, 48, 74, 79, 80, 123
Oldenberg, Margaret, 112
Olesen, Anna Dickie, 121
Olesen, Peter, 121
Olson, Anna, 105
Our Lady of the Sacred Heart Church, 69, 74, 82, 97

P
Paine, J. M., 51, 53
Palki, Erick, 39
Palmer, Finley, 109
Pastika, Joseph, 129
Pederson, Haugbert, 67
Pickle Factory, 48
PINE KNOT, THE, 60, 68
Pleasant Valley, 45
Presbyterian Church of Cloquet, 69

R
Raiter, Roscoe O., 137
Rebecca Lodge, 87
Rengo, Emil, 82
Renwick, Shaw and Crosset Company, 52
Rogstead family, 25
Roley, Bob, 44
Rotary Club of Cloquet, 131
Rousain, E., 16
Rousain, Frank, 16
Roy, Frank 16
Roy, Peter, 16
Roy, Vincent, 16

S
Salo, 67, 80
Samuelson, Julius, 68

Sanborn, Elton, 68
Sauntry and Cain, 59
Sawyer, 15, 18, 66, 80
Scanlon, 25, 28, 37, 46, 53, 62, 67, 68, 72, 81, 137
Scheibe, Clarence, 129
Schlavine, Frank, 26
Shaw Memorial Library, 75
Shaw town, 68
Shaw, George S., 52
Shaw, Mr., 12
Siemer, Minnie, 64
Sioux, 16, 79
Skelly's Orchestra, 114
Skelton, Pearl, 64
Smith, McKean, 108
Solem, Helen Louise, 89
Soo Line, (or Minneapolis, St. Paul and Sault Ste. Marie), 31, 32, 33, 66, 67, 94, 103
Split Rock township 81, 94, 99
St. Casimir's Catholic Church, 81, 82
St. Patrick's Church, 18
St. Paul and Duluth Railroad, 16
Stickney, Mrs., 20
Sts. Mary and Joseph, 18
Syrjala, William, 133
Syverson, Segrid, 85

T
Thomson, 20, 30, 42, 51, 54, 55, 61, 62, 65, 77, 79, 80, 90
Treaty of 1854, 16, 19
Treaty of Fond du Lac, 17
Turpeinen, Viola, 133
Twin Lakes, 28, 126

U
U.S. Railroad Administration, 103
United Brotherhood of Carpenters and Jointers, 134, 135

V
Vasanoja, Saima, 85
Viking Chorus, 106, 114
Viljanen, Emma, 79

W
Walli, Isaac, 82
Walters, F. R., Dr., 87
Walters, Royal, 86
Washington School, 74
Watkins family, 41
Watkins, F. A. Judge, 36
Watkins, Marie, 112
Watkins, Winona, 69, 112
Webber, Mr., 12
Weyerhaeuser, 53, 120
Weyerhaeuser, Frederick, 52
Weyerhaeuser, Rudolph M., 94
Wold, Edward, 42
Wold, Hannah, 42
Wold, Lee, 42
Wold, Lindy, 42
Wood Conversion Company, 62, 120
Woodworth, Annie Mae, 112
Wournos, John, 47
Wrenshall Elementary School, 76
Wrenshall, 25, 26, 30, 41, 45, 52, 53, 63, 66, 81, 91, 107, 110, 115, 122
Wright, 52, 66, 82, 88, 116

Z
Ziebler, Augusta, 33, 81
Ziebler, Charles, 81
Ziebler, Hotel, 33, 81
Zion Lutheran Church, 84

ABOUT THE AUTHORS

FRANCIS M. CARROLL ❦ was born and grew up in Cloquet, Minnesota. He was educated at Carleton College, the University of Minnesota, and Trinity College Dublin, and he is currently a professor of history at the University of Manitoba. He has written or edited five books, including CROSSROADS IN TIME: A HISTORY OF CARLTON COUNTY, MINNESOTA, and, with Franklin R. Raiter, THE FIRES OF AUTUMN: THE CLOQUET-MOOSE LAKE DISASTER OF 1918.

PHOTOGRAPH: *University of Manitoba*

MARLENE WISURI ❦ is the Director of the Carlton County Historical Society. She has graduate degrees from the University of Wisconsin-Superior and the University of Massachusetts-Dartmouth and has taught photography and photo history at several colleges and universities. Her photographs have been exhibited in numerous one-person and group exhibitions. Her previously published works include DOVETAILED CORNERS, a collaborative work of poetry and photography.

PHOTOGRAPH: *Kathryn Nordstrom, Studio One*